Editor-in-Chief and Founder:
  Lyndon H. LaRouche, Jr.
Editorial Board: *Lyndon H. LaRouche, Jr. , Helga
  Zepp-LaRouche, Robert Ingraham, Tony
  Papert, Gerald Rose, Dennis Small, Jeffrey
  Steinberg, William Wertz*
Co-Editors: *Robert Ingraham, Tony Papert*
Technology: *Marsha Freeman*
Transcriptions: *Katherine Notley*
Ebooks: *Richard Burden*
Graphics: *Alan Yue*
Photos: *Stuart Lewis*
Circulation Manager: *Stanley Ezrol*

INTELLIGENCE DIRECTORS
Economics: *Marcia Merry Baker, Paul Gallagher*
History: *Anton Chaitkin*
Ibero-America: *Dennis Small*
Russia and Eastern Europe: *Rachel Douglas*
United States: *Debra Freeman*

INTERNATIONAL BUREAUS
Bogotá: *Miriam Redondo*
Berlin: *Rainer Apel*
Copenhagen: *Tom Gillesberg*
Lima: *Sara Madueño*
Melbourne: *Robert Barwick*
Mexico City: *Gerardo Castilleja Chávez*
New Delhi: *Ramtanu Maitra*
Paris: *Christine Bierre*
Stockholm: *Ulf Sandmark*
United Nations, N.Y.C.: *Leni Rubinstein*
Washington, D.C.: *William Jones*
Wiesbaden: *Göran Haglund*

ON THE WEB
e-mail: eirns@larouchepub.com
www.larouchepub.com
www.executiveintelligencereview.com
www.larouchepub.com/eiw
Webmaster: *John Sigerson*
Assistant Webmaster: *George Hollis*
Editor, Arabic-language edition: *Hussein Askary*

EIR (ISSN 0273-6314) *is published weekly
(50 issues), by EIR News Service, Inc.,
P.O. Box 17390, Washington, D.C. 20041-0390.
(703) 297-8434*

European Headquarters: E.I.R. GmbH, Postfach
Bahnstrasse 9a, D-65205, Wiesbaden, Germany
Tel: 49-611-73650
Homepage: http://www.eir.de
e-mail: info@eir.de
Director: Georg Neudecker

Montreal, Canada: 514-461-1557
eir@eircanada.ca

Denmark: EIR - Danmark, Sankt Knuds Vej 11,
basement left, DK-1903 Frederiksberg, Denmark.
Tel.: +45 35 43 60 40, Fax: +45 35 43 87 57. e-mail:
eirdk@hotmail.com.

Mexico City: EIR, Sor Juana Inés de la Cruz 242-2
Col. Agricultura C.P. 11360
Delegación M. Hidalgo, México D.F.
Tel. (5525) 5318-2301
eirmexico@gmail.com

Copyright: ©2018 EIR News Service. All rights
reserved. Reproduction in whole or in part without
permission strictly prohibited.

Canada Post Publication Sales Agreement
#40683579

Postmaster: Send all address changes to *EIR*, P.O.
Box 17390, Washington, D.C. 20041-0390.

Signed articles in *EIR* represent the views of the authors,
and not necessarily those of the Editorial Board.

Three Presidents Against the British Empire

Trump and Putin Are Making Peace! Important Lessons for the Whole World

by Helga Zepp-LaRouche, Chairwoman of the German political party
Büso, the Civil Rights Solidarity Party

July 21—It ought to be obvious to any thinking person that improving the U.S.-Russia relationship, the relationship between two nations that hold over 90% of the world's nuclear weapons, whose use would wipe out humanity, is a good thing. Therefore, Presidents Trump and Putin absolutely deserve credit for having paved the way, at the Helsinki Summit, for overcoming the current crisis between those two countries through dialogue and cooperation. However, given the unprecedented hysteria of the neoliberal establishment in the United States and the mainstream media on both sides of the Atlantic, in response to this summit, it also becomes clear that this power elite is willing to accept the destruction of human civilization rather than agree to cooperation with Russia.

This reality urgently requires a reassessment of the strategic situation—not only, but especially in European nations such as Germany, where the population has an image of Trump shaped (for example) by reports on Trump on ARD television where 98% of the coverage is negative, and where the demonization of Putin is now part of the "group think" of the local establishment.

The fact is that about half of American voters elected Trump as President, not least because he had promised in his election campaign that he would put the relationship between the United States and Russia back on a sound footing, after it had been brought to an unprecedented, historic low-point by the administrations of George W. Bush and above all Barack Obama. Trump commented on this situation by saying that it was primarily due to American foolishness, for which observation the pseudonymous Publius Tacitus provides detailed arguments at *Sic Semper Tyrannis*, the blog of the renowned security analyst Pat Lang. Regarding the accusation of Russian "interference" in the 2016 election, Publius Tacitus writes that the United States has a long, blood-soaked history of intervention in other countries and the overthrow of elected governments. Regarding the allegation of hacking, he pointed out that the United States, with the CIA, NSA and the Pentagon itself, has the largest and most robust computer networking and hacking capabilities in the world. So those making the accusation live in the biggest damn glass houses.

One of the most interesting effects of the hysteria with which the U.S. establishment has reacted to Trump's attempt to normalize relations with Russia is that the structures of the so-called "deep state" have become transparent. When John Brennan, CIA chief during the Obama administration, accuses Trump of high treason at Helsinki, then of course the question arises as to who or what is allegedly being betrayed. The American people? The American Constitution? Since when is it high treason when the President tries to ensure the physical survival of his own people through a policy of diplomacy and dialogue?

What causes this establishment and its "presstitutes" (as Paul Craig Roberts calls mainstream media representatives) to go off the rails, is that Trump's election victory has shaken the foundations of the neoliberal Anglo-American Empire. Trump promised in his election campaign that he would improve relations with Russia and end the policy of wars of intervention. With the two historic summits of Singapore and Helsinki, he has demonstrated, despite the establishment's enormous resistance, that he is keeping these promises.

The editor of the blog *Antiwar.com*, Justin Raimondi, commented under the title, "Trump's 'Treason': Challenging the Empire," that *"The utter malevolence of our political class was dramatized in all its darkness by their reaction to the Helsinki summit."* Ordinary Americans don't think like elite Americans, he said, who see themselves as the guardians of the international order, a role inherited from the British. "Trump's foreign policy mission (whether he knows it or not) is to eviscerate the outmoded structures—and prejudices—of the Cold War era, and inaugurate a new era in our relations with the rest of the planet."

The international response to the Helsinki Summit signals that most countries see in it the manifestation of a new order. Chinese Foreign Ministry spokeswoman Hua Chunying welcomed the meeting; China, she said, is glad to see an improvement in the relationship between Russia and the United States, which is conducive to world peace and helps the international community to face common challenges together. Israeli Prime Minister Netanyahu welcomed the summit, as did German Chancellor Angela Merkel, who emphasized that these meetings should become normal and that it was "good for everyone" that the next meeting was already planned. Italian Interior Minister Salvini welcomed the rapprochement and described it as good for Italy and Europe.

Whether the hope can be fulfilled of overcoming the Cold War mentality (which can quickly lead to a hot war), and the establishment of a new, better world order, depends critically on the outcome of the war between the U.S. establishment and Trump. The latest episodes in this fight include the U.S. Justice Department's indictment of twelve members of Russian military intelligence, who were accused, literally on the eve of Helsinki, of interfering in the U.S. election, in an obvious attempt to poison the climate for the summit. The well-known Harvard law professor Alan Dershowitz condemned this as a terrible mistake by the Justice Department, which is not supposed to influence foreign policy.

During the joint press conference with Trump in Helsinki, Putin demonstrated that he is a master of the principle of the flank. He invited Special Counsel Robert Mueller, the spearhead of the U.S. establishment, to Russia so that his team could interview these twelve military intelligence officers there, in return for the right of Russian investigators to interview former U.S. Ambassador Michael McFaul and Bill Browder, who was convicted in absentia for tax evasion in Russia—a major contributor to Hillary Clinton's election campaign and responsible for the drafting of the Magnitsky Act. Russia also wanted to interview "former" MI6 agent Christopher Steele, a business partner of Browder, and author of the infamous Trump dossier which formed the basis for the entire staging of the ongoing coup attempt against Trump.

Such a collaborative inquiry would be the only way out of the realm of mutual accusation, and an enlightening exercise in clarifying the truth, as you would inevitably come across the role of British intelligence in the coup attempt against Trump—the secret memoranda of the British GCHQ surveillance apparatus to Obama with the request to monitor Trump Tower, and the entire, extremely professional operation of Christopher Steele to manipulate the 2016 election campaign. There you would find the evidence of the collusion of the Obama administration's intelligence chiefs with MI6 in a coup attempt against the elected U.S. President.

Only four days after Putin's proposal, amidst hysteria over Trump's alleged betrayal, the U.S. Senate voted by a stunning 98 to 0, to prohibit such reciprocal investigations. Ambassador McFaul, who is not only credited with close ties to Browder, but also with active involvement in a policy of regime change against Putin, presented himself as a martyr to Russian attacks, from which the 98 senators, in a sick display of so-called patriotism, had to protect him. But that's not the end of the story. The role of British intelligence and of numerous FBI and Justice Department personnel continues to be the subject of investigations in the Congress and by Trump's lawyers and accused Russians. Some judges have already called for prison sentences for these people.

And then there is the all-important question in America: "How will this play in Peoria?"—"Peoria" being a metaphor for the Great Midwest of the United States, which has a very different political spectrum than the two coasts or Washington inside the Beltway. The majority of the citizens of these states chose Trump because they have been the victims of U.S. establishment policy, and not least because they want a better relationship with Russia. The congressional midterm elections in November will bring this to light.

This domestic political debate in the United States has the most direct implications for the whole world. Should Trump prevail, then, despite the current tensions with China over the U.S. trade deficit, there is a chance for a whole new international policy among the nations of the world, based on recognition of sovereignty, non-intervention in each other's internal affairs, dialogue and mutual benefit. If Trump's opponents prevail, we are probably not far from World War III. So it's time for supporters of "progressive," "left," and "liberal" politics, who have been in the same boat with the CIA, FBI, and MI6 since Trump's election, to reflect on whether the mainstream media have not nudged them into the wrong corner.

Shocking Illegality of FBI's Warrant To Spy on Carter Page

by Bruce Director

July 22—A heavily redacted version of the FBI's request for a Foreign Intelligence Surveillance Act (FISA) warrant on Carter Page, was released July 21, confirming what had already been widely reported, that the FBI's sole pretext for initiating surveillance of Donald Trump's 2016 Presidential campaign, was British intelligence's infamous Steele dossier, which was paid for by Trump's Democratic Party opponent, Hillary Clinton.

The gravamen of the scandal—that the Obama FBI and Justice Department would take action against their political opponents on behalf of a foreign power (Britain)—had already been presented in the House Intelligence Committee's report earlier this year. Nevertheless, the FISA warrant application, when viewed in the context of the DOJ Inspector General's report, and the insane backlash against President Trump's summit with President Putin, lays bare for the American people to see, exactly how corrupt, Obama, Comey, Strzok, McCabe, et al., are.

The application states categorically that Page was a knowing agent of Russia seeking to influence politics in America. The sole basis for the allegation cited in the application is the Steele dossier and news reports based on leaks of the Steele dossier by Christopher Steele himself. Though the FBI knew that the dossier was paid for by the Clinton campaign, it told the Foreign Intelligence Surveillance Court (FISC) only that there was "speculation" that the funders of the report were seeking to gather dirt on a campaign.

Of particular note is the "evidence" of Russian interference in U.S. politics cited on page 21 of the application: that Trump's campaign "worked behind the scenes to make sure Political Party #1 platform would not call for giving weapons to Ukraine to fight Russian and rebel forces, contradicting the view of almost all Political Party #1's foreign policy leaders in Washing-

EDITORIAL

ton." Also cited are news articles criticizing Trump for taking a "milder" tone regarding Russia's "annexation" of Crimea.

Using a political debate about the platform of a political party to justify the intervention of the national security apparatus of the government to control that debate, is as egregious a violation of the First Amendment to the U.S. Constitution as can be found.

Furthermore, the London/Obama Ukraine operation was at the center of the British Empire's strategy to weaken Russia, provoke confrontation, and prevent cooperation between the United States and Russia—now being pursued by Trump, with much opposition from Britain and its operatives in the United States. The central role this played in the FISA warrant application shows that this wasn't a matter of "partisan" politics, but of grand strategy.

President Trump addressed this in several tweets this morning: "Source #1 was the (Fake) Dossier. Yes, the Dirty Dossier, paid for by Democrats as a hit piece against Trump, and looking for information that could discredit Candidate #1 Trump. Carter Page was just the foot to surveil the Trump campaign.... ILLEGAL!"

And again: "This is so bad that they should be looking at the judges who signed off on this stuff, not just the people who gave it. It is so bad it screams out at you. On the whole FISA scam which led to the rigged Mueller Witch Hunt!"

His third tweet was: "Congratulations to @JudicialWatch and @TomFitton on being successful in getting the Carter Page FISA documents. As usual they are ridiculously heavily redacted but confirm with little doubt that the Department of 'Justice' and FBI misled the courts. Witch Hunt Rigged, a Scam!"

And finally, "I had a GREAT meeting with Putin and the Fake News used every bit of their energy to try and disparage it. So bad for our country!"

EIR Contents

www.larouchepub.com   Volume 45, Number 30, July 27, 2018

Channel 90 Seconds TV

Cover This Week

Presidents Putin, Trump and Xi at the APEC summit in Vietnam, Nov. 11, 2017. Vietnamese President Tran Dai Quang is to the right of Trump.

THREE PRESIDENTS AGAINST THE BRITISH EMPIRE

Farm Belt Fighter: 'Restore the American System and American Culture Now!'

The following is an interview with Ron Wieczorek, an Independent candidate in South Dakota running for U.S. Congress, conducted July 20, 2018 by EIR's Robert Baker.

EIR: You've been a fighter in the farm belt for years in South Dakota for the policies of Lyndon LaRouche, and the economic policies that made America a great nation. I understand this is your third run for Congress. It's not as if you don't have other things to do, raising Charolais cattle, selling bulls and otherwise working in agriculture. Why do this again?

Wieczorek: Back in the 1980s, I had been a Massey-Ferguson implement dealer for a number of years, when Fed Chairman Paul Volcker and President Jimmy Carter took the Prime Rate to 22%. From 1980-1984, I saw one-third of my farm customers go out of business in the ensuing crisis. I was involved in taking testimony on the effects on ordinary farmers of this high interest-rate regime, and in many cases succeeded in getting the Federal Housing Administration to grant moratoria on farm foreclosures.

What we're experiencing right now is very similar, and I actually expect it to become worse that it was then, if we don't get some things done very soon. That's one of the reasons I'm running for Congress. The other reason is that I'm very concerned for our young people. We've got a misconception of what Free Trade has done

Yankton Press & Dakotan/ Kelly Hertz

Ron Wieczorek, Independent candidate for U.S. Congress.

to this country, and we need an educational process to get people reoriented to the American political-economic system.

British Free Trade vs. the American System

EIR: How do you explain Free Trade to people?

Wieczorek: All they have to do is look at the current economic situation. Twenty-five years of Free Trade has devastated this country and all of the nations that have participated in it, especially the Atlantic Alliance countries of Europe and North America. Twenty-five years of Free Trade has created a post-industrial society. It's destroyed most of the family farmers in North Dakota. For example, there are only seven dairy farms left in the state. The crisis that the Ag sector in general and dairy farmers in particular are facing is mind-boggling. The eaters are the ones I'm really concerned about, because we're about to have a food crisis.

The change of the economic policies in our education system to a Free Trade oriented approach, vs. what we had before, has allowed our manufacturing to be moved out of the country, destroyed our labor unions, and destroyed the national sovereignty of a lot of the nations of the world. We've destroyed the credit system that this country was built on.

EIR: I know that you have concentrated on what is known as LaRouche's Four Laws. I think a lot of people confuse the American System of Economics up with the British Free Trade system. Could you tell our readers some about the key elements in LaRouche's Four Laws?

Wieczorek: The restoration of the original 1933 Glass-Steagall Banking Act by Congress and its reimplementation as law again is absolutely essential. That's the Number One thing that needs to be done. In 2013, I was responsible for organizing the South Dakota State Legislature to be the first state legislature in the nation to unanimously pass a Resolution calling on the U.S. Congress to reinstate the 1930s-era Glass-Steagall Act. I'm proud to say that the original Glass-Steagall Act was passed with the help of one of South Dakota's best Senators, Peter Norbeck.

In 1971 President Nixon took the nation off the gold reserve standard and the fixed exchange rate system established at Bretton Woods in 1944, and allowed the currencies of nations to float freely with respect to each other. As a result, the value of the dollar against the other currencies now changes almost by the second. When you think about it, it would be pretty darn hard to build a barn if you had to change your ruler every minute, or every day, even! We need long-term stability back in our currency. We need serious regulation of the banking system again. Separating the commercial banks from the investment banks is absolutely essential to maintaining a stable economic system.

And then, of course, we have to have a national banking system. A national bank, or some form of credit-generating institution, such as President Franklin Roosevelt set up with the Reconstruction Finance Corporation. A Commodity Credit Corporation will also be absolutely essential to getting stability back in the farm area, considering the fall-off in prices and the lost markets, due to sanctions that were put on a number of years ago. The sanctioned countries aren't going to let their people starve to death. We have destroyed our own agriculture sector, at least the family-farmer, by moving to corporate farming, industrial farming. The poor animals are penned and treated like they're not even living creatures. It's horrible what we've tolerated and done here.

There's another reason why I am running for Congress. My great grandson, an eighth generation Ameri-

Deanna Wieczorek

Candidate Wieczorek campaigning to rebuild America.

can, was just born recently, and he deserves a future. I think I made a mistake not voting for Donald Trump. I think this man is very concerned about leaving a legacy that could make him one of the greatest presidents we've had, if he moves right. I need to get to Washington to help him move in the right direction. He needs to follow me! It's time to listen to LaRouche.

A Hamiltonian Credit System

EIR: A lot of people think of credit and money as sort of the same thing. You're saying we've got to get, instead, a *credit* system. Could you discuss the difference?

Wieczorek: Almost 55 years ago, when I first started farming, I had a man who agreed to rent a half-section of land—320 acres. I had a grandfather who told me that if I helped him, he would let me use his equipment to farm that land. I didn't have any money. I was 18 years old in high school yet. I went to the grain elevator operator, telling him that I needed seed oats enough to plant 160 acres. They extended me the credit to put in the oats, with an agreement that when I harvested, I would come in to the elevator, sell the oats, and pay him back.

I did the same thing with the seed corn company. United Hagie had a program that was interest-free until October, so I got seed corn to plant. My gas man also

Wieczorek in interview with Todd Epp for KELO Talk News Radio.

gave me credit. The company charged me no interest. It was a credit system back then.

Today, any young man trying to do what I did back then, will pay 18% interest after 30 days! That's not a credit system! Farmers and business people and the small towns were making a hell of lot more money back in the 1950s, even into the 1960s, and were a lot more successful than they are today. Today, there's nothing left of most of our small towns. Recently I found myself on Main Street in Marion (pop. 784 in 2010). Peering into the window of a clothing store, I just cried. The manikins were clothed, but the clothing was faded and all falling off. The racks were still there, but everything was covered with dust. The store must have closed 10-15 years ago. Nothing has changed in Marion during all these years, except that so many have lost their livelihoods and their lives.

Under Free Trade, we've had probably 20 years of stagnant wages—actually probably a decline in wages. People now have to have two or three jobs to maintain a family. It's not only the farmers who are getting hit; it's the laboring man also. While the Wall Streeters are busy squirreling away their so-called profits, at the same time they're indebting the nation deeper and deeper, because we're creating so little new tangible wealth.

Moving all our production to the least-cost areas of the world, is nothing but a looting system, and when you loot your fellow man and your fellow country, how do you expect them to be able to buy your products? The only thing you can do is keep lowering and lowering the prices of your products until *everybody* is collapsed. It's a system of mutual destruction.

Infrastructure

EIR: I know your campaign put up a huge billboard just east of Sioux Falls on I-90. It's got a picture on it of a magnetic levitation train. Why are you promoting that?

Wieczorek: Several reasons. We need major infrastructure for the future. If we're going to be a world that's going to get along, we need to be helping other countries. With the Bering Strait tunnel, and mag-lev trains all over North and South America, Asia, Europe and Africa, and even the possibility of tying into Australia some day, every continent in the world could be connected, in a peaceful way. Rather than using just the rivers and the oceans as a means of transportation, this extensive rail network will be much better, as it provides the potential for development *all along the routes*. We will build new cities along those corridors of development.

Along with high-speed rail, we're going to need water development. The North American Water and Power Alliance (NAWAPA) project that President John Kennedy supported clear back in the 1960s, to bring water down from the Yukon and Mackenzie rivers in Alaska, should have been built a long time ago. That massive water management project will generate the electricity for the rail system. You can't get any environmentally cleaner power than electricity produced by hydro, nuclear, or (in the future) fusion.

Creating construction jobs to build all this is no different than what Alexander Hamilton and President George Washington did with road and canal building. It's the same as what President Abraham Lincoln did with the Homestead Act and the trans-continental railroad. We haven't done anything like this since the 1970s. Free Trade doesn't tolerate such development because the speculators have a system in which they can make more money in half an hour, than on a 50-year financing of hydro-electric system.

EIR: In your discussions around the state, you've stressed the importance of culture, of education. A recent joint study by the American Farm Bureau and the National Farmers Union reports that the number one concern of farmers is opioids. How are you giving people hope?

Wieczorek: Again, I'm going to knock Free Trade, because it's the evil here. Free Trade looks at Man as a commodity for cheap labor. That's as far as the concern goes: getting as much work out of the individual as possible. That's not what this country was about. We use technology produced by our minds to make things more efficient and more prosperous. That pursuit is supposed to free up Man, so he can have a cultural life to enjoy.

Culture and Education

In America, we don't have that culture anymore. It's now totally entertainment; it's not based on a culture that uplifts and develops the human mind. It's a culture that wastes our time. Turn on your TV and tune in to this athletic mentality. You've got twenty millionaires running around fields chasing bags of hot air. What kind of culture is that? We should have choruses for all our young people, where they can develop their minds.

Actually, if you learn to sing properly, at a very early age your mind learns how to control your vocal chords. Singing teaches you lawfulness and orderliness. I really think that people with a proper classical education will automatically do the right thing 90% of time, because you're training your subconscious. That's what education should be about. The subconscious, your mind, is the part of you that has the potential to exist for ever, if used properly, in the ideas that you pass on to others—the ideas that you generate with that thing between your ears—I mean, that's a terribly important thing. In America today, we're wasting that most beautiful and natural resource.

I truly feel sorry for the kids today, with the education system we have, which is focused solely on creating laborers for a workforce, rather than developing the human mind in the proper direction. We've simply got to overhaul our educational process. I think I got a better education in a one-room schoolhouse (located on my grandfather's property, by the way), because of the effects of a classical education back then, than my kids are getting in these ungodly, overbuilt school systems

Jenny Burns

Talking with students in the cafeteria at Dakota State University in Madison.

Gathering signatures at the Benson Flea Market in Sioux Falls.

Deanna Wieczorek

of today, with all that money spent on athletic fields. I'm not against athletics, but when you monetize it, there's something wrong with it.

EIR: You told the *Yankton Daily Press & Dakotan* recently that in 1991, during the economic embargo against Iraq, you worked with the Committee to Save the Children in Iraq. You warned at that time that we had better change our policy, or we would see a massive disruption clear across the Middle East.

Wieczorek: Yes. Along with 19 other American dairy farmers from eight states working to save these children from starvation, I personally organized two tons of milk powder to be transported to Baghdad. I didn't want my children and grandchildren to be enemies of the Iraqis. I totally agreed with what LaRouche said at that time that wars of aggression should never be part of the American System. Food absolutely should never be used as a weapon. That's about as evil as you can get, as far as I'm concerned: to starve innocent young people and the elderly. I don't know how much less merciful you could be than doing something like that.

We need to get along with people. Economics has to

Jeannie Hockett

Wieczorek and his wife Deanna share a moment with Eleanor and Franklin Roosevelt at Hyde Park, New York, July 2017.

be looked at more as a method by which you house and clothe and feed, and otherwise care for more and more people at a higher and higher standard of living. It's a science, not a looting process. We have to get over the idea that somebody has to lose, so somebody else can win. We need to go back to the American System, where you had a win-win situation—what FDR intended to do for Africa, and with the Marshall Plan of rebuilding all of Europe. When we rebuilt Europe, we made prosperous the people there who could then purchase our manufactured products after we had built the greatest manufacturing process in the world to save us from Nazi Germany.

The reason I'm a big LaRouche supporter, is because Lyn represents the Constitution of the United States in the most dramatic and best way that it can possibly be represented. In the 1992 Presidential campaign, I brought more delegates for Lyndon LaRouche to the South Dakota Democratic Party State Convention than Bill Clinton had. Stupidly, the Democrat party disqualified several of the LaRouche delegates.

South Dakota

I started out my adult life as an Abraham Lincoln Republican, then switched to an FDR and JFK Democrat, and am now an Independent. When the parties changed their principles, I changed parties. Lincoln, FDR, and JFK would all be in the LaRouche organization today. Much of China is moving in the proper direction. They're on the LaRouche team. They're using LaRouche's policies. Russia is the same way. Leading Russians know more about the American System than the most Americans do today.

The educational process that I'm pushing to get

through, is part of the LaRouche program. It's an absolute must, if we're going to turn this nation around and become the great and wonderful, beautiful and respected leaders that we were at one point.

EIR: How are South Dakotans reacting to your campaign?

Wieczorek: I'm getting a lot of positive feedback! In the process of campaigning, I usually try to point out the fight between the Republic and the Empire systems. That's something that has to be acknowledged. If you look at the Empire systems of the world, they've always ended after about 200 years, or maybe a little bit longer. This country, however, was built on the new principles of a republic, where the purpose of the government was to uplift and develop the human mind and the productive powers of its citizens.

An empire system is a few people at the top enslaving, and otherwise taking advantage of their fellow men to try to get ahead. Many of the people I am speaking to quickly understand the difference between what our former government was, and what it is today. If we let this continue much longer, the United States is going to be the empire that's going to collapse. It's not the enemy from without that's destroying our minds and the concepts and methods of the American political-economic system; it's the enemy from within.

EIR: President Trump has done some pretty interesting things recently, including meeting with Russia's President Putin. What do you say about that, and the massive post-summit attacks against Trump?

Wieczorek: I'm totally supportive of President Trump's efforts to bring peace to the world. I appreciate what he accomplished in his meeting in Singapore with Kim Jong-un of North Korea, his getting along with President Xi Jinping of China, and his latest meeting with Russia's President Vladimir Putin in Helsinki. He has probably done the best that he *could* do by doing what he *has* done.

Trump's opposition in the United States is based on the system of empire. I cannot believe what's happened to the Democratic Party. It's turned away from being the party of the working man and the family farmer, to the party of the Wall Street fraudster or bankster, as FDR would refer to them. They've forgotten who Roosevelt and Kennedy were. These Presidents were generators of peace. Even during the Cold War they communicated with Russia.

Some of these lunatics who are running their mouths off, condemning the President for meeting with Putin, are using the word "treason." That's a very stiff word. I think that a lot of these people screaming "Treason!" are in fact themselves the treasoners. These people are sticking their necks out a very long way. I hope the ropes don't slip off. Truth and Justice will win in the end, but I hope our country is not destroyed in the process. I hope we can get a turnaround, before we get a civil war.

We Need Honest People To Use Their Minds

EIR: What is your next step?

Wieczorek: I have three opponents: a Libertarian former police officer who's a medical marijuana activist, a Democrat former state court judge, and a Republican former chairman of the South Dakota Public Utilities Commission. All three have worked in some capacity or other for the government all their lives. *We don't need more bureaucrats in Washington!* If we're going to "drain the swamp," we need to get rid of the bureaucrats and get some ordinary and honest people up there who have some experience and some concepts, and are willing and able to use their minds.

I'm 75 years old, and probably shouldn't be doing what I'm doing, but nobody else from this area is doing it. I really feel that I have done my homework. I know what needs to be done. I've had experience in agribusiness. I've been a farmer. I'm a member of the Farmers Union and National Farmers Organization. I've been a political organizer. Over the past twenty-five years or so, I have participated in many international conferences convened to promote the construction of infrastructure and general economic development.

I've been an advocate for the "forgotten man," you might say, watching one-third of my customers going out of business back in the 1980s, and seeing all those suicides. The last time I looked, the suicide rate among farmers was higher than it was at any time during the 1980s, as far as percentage of farmers. We don't have many farmers left. I doubt if we've got half a million actual family-farmers left.

So, we haven't got much time to reverse this policy and get this country back up and going again. Maybe we need this collapse to bring down some of these giant

Bob Baker

Wieczorek, aged 75, in trademark black Stetson, bolo tie, black vest and red shirt, turns in 4,000 signatures to the South Dakota Secretary of State, to qualify for ballot status.

monopolies. I don't know. I think there's a much safer and better way to it, if we can get the public organized around what needs to be done. If they will just stand up and politically fight. That's the only way they're going to get out; they can't get another job; most of them are over-worked already. It's time we stand up together. We have a president that wants to drain the swamp, who's moving in the right direction. I think we just need to send some good people to Washington who appreciate the concepts he's trying to get across.

I really think we have to get LaRouche's ideas more into the public arena. A lot of people are more or less familiar with LaRouche's ideas, and agree with them, but we just need some elected leadership that can take the point on this.

I pledge to work to end the coup against President Donald Trump. We don't need an impeachment crisis. I pledge to work to get the United States to join China's Belt and Road Initiative, as part of a program for general economic recovery, a program for the future peace and prosperity of the United States and the entire world. I will work to get Glass-Steagall reinstated before the impending financial crash renders sensible banking reform unattainable. I believe that the increase in productivity is the metric for the application of credit. We need to fully engage the nation in fusion power realization and space exploration.

I don't expect to be the "miracle man" to change everything, but I certainly believe the ideas I represent can have a major effect on making this a much, much better world.

Dramatic Policy Shift Puts Regional Development at Center Stage

by Douglas DeGroot

July 19—New Ethiopian Prime Minister Abiy Ahmed—only sworn in on April 2—has moved with a rapidity that has surprised Ethiopians and Eritreans, to keep his word on two pledges he made when he was sworn in: to end the drawn-out state of war with neighboring Eritrea; and to end the draconian internal security focus which branded members of opposition groups as terrorists, and sent them to prison.

Abiy is moving rapidly with respect to normalization of relations with Eritrea and aggressive reform of Ethiopia's approach to internal security. These important developments, very significant in themselves, are getting the bulk of the international news coverage.

Xinhua/Michael Tewelde

Ethiopian Prime Minister Abiy Ahmed (with dark glasses) welcoming Eritrean Foreign Minister Osman Salah to Addis Ababa for the first official contact between the two countries in over 20 years.

An Economic Union for the Region

However, before he began implementing these important policy shifts, Abiy was focused on laying the groundwork for ensuring the continued, rapid economic development of Ethiopia—the world's fastest growing economy—and of its immediate neighbors, in a win-win fashion. Abiy undertook visits to Ethiopia's immediate neighbors and several other nations in the region. When he visited Ethiopia's immediate neighbors of Somalia, Djibouti, Sudan, and Kenya, he proposed financial cooperation with each nation to make joint investments and ownership of projects, such as expansion of their ports and transport infrastructure, with the goal of developing the entire Horn of Africa region. These visits demonstrated that the top priority for Ethiopia remains its plan to become the hub of industrialization in Africa, following the development model of China.

Abiy's chief of staff, Fitsun Arega, stated to the *EastAfrican* May 12 that Abiy's goal on the visits was to lay the basis for creating an economic union: "Djibouti, Ethiopia, Kenya, and Sudan will now work towards a true economic union with joint investments and ownership of projects because our people's shared prosperity and security depend on it." Abiy traveled with high-level delegations on each trip.

Ethiopia made a deal to acquire a 19% ownership stake in the Port of Berbera in Somaliland, a region of Somalia that is trying to break away from the Somali government. But Abiy's intention is not to encourage secession. Abiy also offered to participate in four Somali port projects.

Abiy went to Djibouti April 28-29 to meet President Omar Guelleh. They made an agreement for Ethiopia to take an ownership concession in the port, which handles 95% of Ethiopia's inbound trade. In February, Djibouti nationalized the Doraleh Container Terminal there, cancelling DP-World's concession to run the terminal, after a six-year dispute. Since then, Djibouti has had difficulty finding other investors in the facility because the legal wrangling between DP-World and Djibouti made it risky. DP-World is owned by the government of Dubai. In return, Abiy offered Djibouti the possibility of acquiring concessions in Ethiopian state-owned companies.

On May 2-3, Abiy went to Sudan. He made an agreement with President Omar Hassan al-Bashir whereby Ethiopia acquired a concession in Port Sudan. Ethiopian Foreign Ministry spokesman Meles Alem said that the two leaders "agreed to develop Port Sudan together," according to a report in *africannews.com*. They also agreed to build a new railway line from Ethiopia to Khartoum and a trans-border economic zone, and to develop the border town of Assosa into a commercial center.

Abiy went to Kenya May 6-7 for talks with Kenyan President Uhuru Kenyatta. Ethiopia was given rights for formal acquisition of land at the new Port Lamu deep water port to set up a logistics facility. They agreed

Xinhua/Michael Tewelde

Eritrean President Isaias Afwerki (right) and Ethiopian Prime Minister Abiy Ahmed, raising an Eritrean flag as the Eritrean embassy is reopened in the Ethiopian capital of Addis Ababa on July 16, 2018.

to work on joint projects, such as roads and railways. Both sides agreed to jointly invest in the "Moyale Joint City and Economic Zone" project, according to the joint communiqué. Moyale is the main Kenya-Ethiopia border town. The presidents "committed to the development of the Lamu Port-South Sudan-Ethiopia Transport Corridor (LAPSSET); the Northern Corridor including road network between Isiolo [and] Moyale through to Addis Ababa; and the railway from Addis Ababa to Nairobi." (Isiola, in Kenya, is on the route between Lamu Port and the border at Moyale.) The LAPSSET Corridor megaproject is East Africa's largest and most ambitious infrastructure project, bringing together Ethiopia, Kenya, and South Sudan, with the potential to expand to Uganda and Rwanda.

He also visited Uganda, Egypt, Rwanda (often paired with Ethiopia as a similarly minded development economy), and the Gulf states UAE and Saudi Arabia.

Industrialization Perspective

Ethiopia is the second most populous country in Africa, with a population of 102 million. Its economy has been growing at 10% per year for the last ten years. Ethiopia intends to maintain this economic growth rate. At the beginning of the 1990s, its economic growth rate was only 3%. Ethiopia's Vision 2025 plan has as its target rapid economic growth, to make it the leading manufacturing hub in Africa. The plan projects GDP growing by 11% per year and manufacturing growing

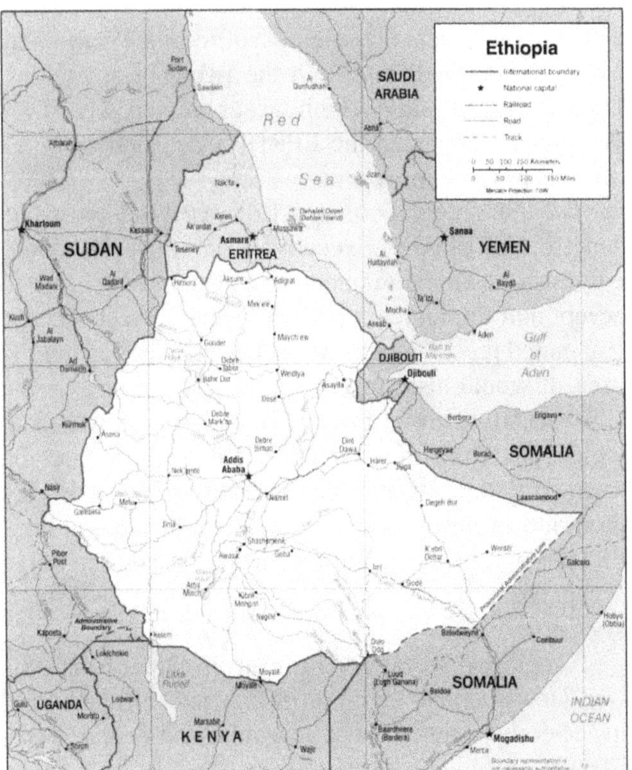

The Addis Ababa to Djibouti all-electric rail line, built in collaboration with China, as it crosses Holhol bridge.

by 25% per year over the next ten years, in the view of Arkebe Oqubay, the architect of Ethiopia's industrial breakout.

Arkebe said in a BBC interview in August 2017 that "Expanding and building world class industrial parks is a model we have chosen." He also pointed out that "the population is growing by about 5% so we need to create close to one million jobs every year." He understands that population is an important resource. He pointed out that "population growth is not only a challenge, but also an opportunity if it's linked with quite rapid economic growth."

To accompany the industrial parks, Ethiopia is building—with China's help—large, affordable apartment blocks, in addition to new road systems. The new electric rail line from Addis Ababa to Djibouti has been completed. As Arkebe pointed out: "We can learn from China that making investment in the long-term, in infrastructure, is quite important. We have seen China emerge from low level, into being a manufacturing powerhouse."

Hawassa Industrial Park, said to be the biggest in Africa, is one of a dozen or more that are being built or have been built in Ethiopia. It covers 140 hectares (350 acres) and will have a workforce of 60,000. It was built by China Civil Engineering Construction Corporation (CCECC) in nine months.

Arkebe made it clear that Ethiopia will not rest on the laurels of its past accomplishments. He stated that "Building democracies, and sustaining them, requires effort for many generations, and we recognize that, and

we are going to put more effort despite the achievements we have made."

Half of the adult population is illiterate, according to reports, and 80% are rural. Rapid industrialization and the ongoing push for education will continually lower these percentages.

Ethiopia now has only enough reserves for two months' worth of imports. To be able to keep spending at the rate required for its ambitious development program, it is now going to sell stakes in some of its state-run businesses, to generate more funds.

Internal Policy Shift

The Ethiopian Peoples' Revolutionary Democratic Front (EPRDF) has ruled Ethiopia since defeating the bloody Derg regime of Haile Mariam Mengistu in 1991. After its popular first prime minister, Meles Zenawi, died in 2012, Hailemariam Desalegn became prime minister until he suddenly resigned on Feb. 15, 2018. The last three years of his term in office were marked by extensive political unrest in the two largest regions, Oromia and Amhara, which he suppressed. These developments preceded the EPRDF's decision to select Abiy as prime minister.

The issue of relations with Eritrea was addressed on June 5. The EPRDF Executive Committee unexpectedly issued a communiqué, stating that it had decided to accept and implement the 2000 Algiers Peace Accord that ended the 29-month war between Ethiopia and Eritrea. It would also implement the 2002 ruling by the UN-backed Eritrea-Ethiopia Boundary Commission, which gave to Eritrea some disputed territories and the town of Badme, where the conflict originated. Eighty thousand or more troops were killed during that conflict. Prior to that time, Ethiopian policy had been not to accept the rulings of the Algiers Accord and the Boundary Commission.

It took two weeks for Eritrean President Isaias Afwerki to respond to this surprise announcement. He said in a speech on June 20 that he would send Foreign Minister Osman Saleh and Afwerki's right hand man, Yemane

Xinhua/Michael Tewelde

Partial view of Hawassa Industrial Park, the largest in Africa at this point, 275 kilometers south of Addis Ababa.

Gebreab, to visit Addis. As a result of this visit, Abiy made a trip to Eritrea for a direct meeting with Afwerki.

Afwerki traveled to Addis Ababa a week later, on July 14. He re-established relations with Ethiopia. After his return, Eritrean troops were pulled back from the border and 35 people who had been detained on religious grounds, were released by Eritrea.

Two months ahead of schedule, Abiy lifted the state of emergency that had been imposed when Abiy's predecessor, Prime Minister Hailemariam Desalegn, had resigned. Abiy also freed political prisoners. At the historic summit on July 8 with Afwerki in the Eritrean capital, Asmara, he signed a declaration ending the state of war between the two countries. This move was met with enthusiasm and tearful reunions on both sides of the border.

Eritrea seceded from Ethiopia in 1993. After the war, the two countries had a rigid focus on internal security. Political opposition groups in Ethiopia were given sanctuary in Eritrea. Both countries were dominated by security concerns. Eritrea had a policy of mandatory army conscription for an indefinite period of time. Many fled the country to escape being in the army for an undetermined period. As a result, more of the refugees fleeing to Europe from Africa came from Eritrea, which has a population of only 5 million, than from any other single African country.

As part of his policy reversal, Abiy has publicly stated that branding opposition groups as terrorists and putting their members in prison, was a form of state terrorism. He has released and pardoned these political prisoners, after his meetings with Afwerki in Eritrea and in the Ethiopian capital of Addis Ababa on Afwerki's reciprocal visit.

Normalization of relations with Eritrea makes it more likely that the Eritrean ports of Assab and especially Massawa, a container port, can be developed, and transport connections to them upgraded, providing access to the sea, as was the case before secession. During the state dinner hosted by Afwerki in Eritrea on July 8, Abiy said that Ethiopia is ready to use the Eritrean port.

Three armed opposition groups have been removed from the terror list as a result of the reforms. One of the them, the Ogaden National Liberation Front (ONLF), however, has repeated its pledge to disrupt Ethiopian production of oil and gas in the Ogaden region. China's POLY-GCL Petroleum Group Holdings Ltd. is set to start oil tests. Gas reserves are estimated to be 6-8 trillion cubic feet. Plans have been made for a $4 billion project to construct a pipeline to a liquefaction plant to be built in Djibouti. In 2007 a Chinese-run oil field in the Ogaden was attacked by ONLF, killing nine Chinese and 65 Ethiopians. The ONLF was set up in 1984 and was headquartered in Kuwait.

On June 7 Abiy carried out a wide-ranging reshuffle of top security officials. On June 23, in Addis Ababa where he addressed a big rally, a hand grenade was thrown at the platform. Two died, but Abiy escaped injury. The person who threw the grenade wore a police uniform, and came to the location in a police car. The car was torched, preventing any evidence related to the incident from being analyzed.

Ethiopia has already come a long way, if one considers that in the 1950s and 1960s, Ethiopians would prostrate themselves on the ground when Emperor Selassie passed in his black Rolls Royce. Ethiopia still has a lot to accomplish, but it is doing it at only one speed—as fast as possible. People who doubt that Ethiopia can accomplish its goal, are asked by Ethiopians to look at what China did in 40 years.

dougdegroot@larouchepub.com

British Lawn Jockey Obama Seeks a White Horse

by Ramasimong Phillip Tsokolibane, leader of LaRouche South Africa

July 21—On July 17, that loyal servant of the British Empire and its liberal monetarist system, Barack Obama, used the podium of the annual Nelson Mandela Lecture, on the centenary of tata's [Mandela's] birth, to arrogantly claim his mantle, loudly proclaiming his willingness to fight for justice, "democratic values," "human rights," and a more equal distribution of wealth, and in effect offering to lead a global movement to fight for these values. The former U.S. President and full-time British black lawn jockey now seeks his "white horse" to ride—that is, a movement of fools and dupes, whom he will lead to their own slaughter, in an effort to "reform" the liberal monetarist world order. That order cannot be reformed. It must be totally discarded, if mankind is to survive much further into this new millennium.

Judging by the response of the large and cheering crowd that packed Johannesburg's Wanderers sports stadium, his offer and message were well received. His message was not only addressed to South Africans, but, via the mass media, to a global audience.

Perhaps when the air clears a bit, some people may reflect on what he said, and will find it to be so much sophist bullshit, in classy packaging, presented by one of the foremost sophists of our day. Thinking a bit harder, they might see, all over this speech, not an echo of our great leader, but a great hollowness played by a dying British Empire and its bitch Queen—they who would use Obama to put his finger in an already failing dyke, to hold back a truly global revolution that is welling up to wipe away the old failing monetarist order, along with its British Royal masters and such loyal servants as Obama.

Obama tried to put a label on our revolution, calling it reactionary, and saying that this is what we must fear. No Mr. O, it is *precisely* those like you who claim that

White House/Samantha Appleton
Killer Barack Obama receives the Nobel Peace Prize in 2009.

the system can be saved and reformed that we must fear. Reactionaries are present in every revolutionary period. In the end, because they have nothing positive to say about the future, they are swept aside by the revolutionary process itself.

No, it is Obama and his ilk we must fear, because they seek to deceive people into believing that there just might yet be a way to save their sinking selves within the existing paradigm, when this is impossible. They divert people from the true tasks at hand, as they vainly attempt to disrupt and delay the process of revolutionary change, so that their masters might have a chance (as they imagine) to put in place what is needed to slaughter their potential opponents.

The Killer with the Peace Prize

Obama is a liar, a fact known to many Americans, who heard for eight years his lies about wanting to fight the "powers of greed and money," when all he did as President was bail out the big banks and keep the big-time crooks and speculators—who run the banks and other corrupted financial institutions—from being prosecuted. It's no surprise that the Obama Foundation is funded with millions upon millions of dollars from Wall Street and the institutions that protect Wall Street. It is funded not only by Goldman Sachs, but by the Ford Foundation and other foundations that front for Wall Street.

Nobel Peace Prize laureate Barack Obama claims to seek "peace," proclaiming he wants to end the bloodshed in the Middle East and elsewhere. Yet, as President, Obama was the most savage and brutal of leaders, who organized the destruction of nations, such as Syria and Libya, murdered and assassinated leaders, and ordered the deaths of those he claimed were terrorists—without trial, and often without any proof at all. Obama was in reality "the black Bush," whose policies and directions, like the white Bush, left a trail of dead bodies strewn across the planet.

Obama Recruiting Against the BRICS

What Obama *didn't* say, what he deliberately ignored, speaks volumes as to his agentry for, and loyalty to his British masters. There was not one word about the BRICS alliance, which represents the seed crystal of a new global order based on peace through economic development, and whose July 25-27 Summit our nation will host. This is where the true challenge to the existing system lies. In the policies of the One Belt One Road initiative of China there are no losers, only winners; there are no adversaries, only collaborators. No mention of any of this by our self-proclaimed visionary, who did find time, however, to *attack* China and by implication Russia, our nation's most powerful allies, for their allegedly "authoritarian" forms of economics and mercantilist trade policies which, he said, African nations and others are supposed to reject:

> Many developing countries now are looking at China's model of authoritarian control combined with mercantilist capitalism as preferable to the messiness of democracy. Who needs free speech as long as the economy is going good? The free press is under attack. Censorship and state control of media is on the rise. Social media—once seen as a mechanism to promote knowledge and understanding and solidarity—has proved to be just as effective promoting hatred and paranoia and propaganda and conspiracy theories. (Applause)

Africa should reject *what*? Are you crazy—you stupid, arrogant British tool? While you lie about the true content of China and Russia's policy towards the world, you want to drive all of us back into the hands of the masters of the dying monetarist system, which even you admitted is not working so well.

For reasons I have discussed before, there is no possibility of reforming the monetarist system, whose death occurred, in reality, more than 50 years ago, which system has been sustained only at great and unacceptable suffering and death, and by the ability of its British masters and their American allies to extract their "pound of flesh" to support mountains of worthless speculative and other paper "assets." Nevertheless, the British wish to use their black lawn jockey Obama as a sort of Pied Piper who, through clever sophistry, will end up leading those who follow him to their own slaughter when the moment of revolutionary change is at hand.

For him to do so by invoking the name of a true revolutionary, Madiba—as I warned he would—is disgusting and a desecration of Mandela's memory and life's work. It was equally disgusting to see our President and other leaders fawning over Obama, as if he were some deity.

I urge my fellow Patriots not to be diverted by this sophist, but to "keep your eyes on the prize." As I said, the BRICS Summit is now only days away. That is where real history must and will be made, where the pathway to a new global order must be laid out.

Barack Obama and his masters would prefer to make no mention of the BRICS, while they seek to target and destabilize its members—Brazil, Russia, India, China, and our own country, South Africa. They know, even if they don't say it, that the present form of the monetarist order may not survive beyond this year, but they do not want a BRICS challenge to that order.

We should be happy to be alive in a truly revolutionary moment, in which great change is possible—if we ignore false leaders and their sophistry. Change must occur. Change will occur.

Do you have the courage to determine what it will be, and not leave your children's future to livery like Obama, or worse?

Contact the author at ramasimongt@hotmail.com

Leaders of the five member nations at the Ninth BRICS Summit, in China, September 2017 (from left): the Presidents of Brazil, Russia, China, and South Africa, and the Prime Minister of India.

ZEPP-LAROUCHE WEBCAST

Trump-Putin Summit Brings World Closer to New Paradigm

This is the edited transcript of the July 19, 2018 Schiller Institute New Paradigm webcast, an interview with the founder of the Schiller Institutes, Helga Zepp-LaRouche. She was interviewed by Harley Schlanger. A video of the webcast is available.

Harley Schlanger: Hello, I'm Harley Schlanger from the Schiller Institute. Welcome to our webcast this week, featuring our founder Helga Zepp-LaRouche.

Helga, it's only been a couple of days since the summit in Helsinki, and yet it's clear the world has en-tered a new phase of strategic relations. The summit itself was an incredible success, and you can tell that, because immediately, those who had been doing everything they could to sabotage the summit, are now trying to sabotage its results. The President is accurate in characterized their madness as "Trump Derangement Syndrome."

I think it's important we start with what actually happened at the summit, because the media, in their coverage of what they wanted Trump to do and what he didn't do, ignored what actually did happen between

White House/Andrea Hanks

Presidents Trump (left) and Putin hold a joint press conference at the Helsinki Summit on July 16, 2018.

the two Presidents. So, why don't we start there, Helga?

Helga Zepp-LaRouche: Indeed, this was a very historic summit. The fact that the leaders of the two most important nuclear powers of the world have opened up a dialogue between them, is really is important for world peace. As noted by Trump, and also I think by Putin at some point, together they represent countries possessing more than 90% of the world's nuclear weapons. With the promise of many more summits to come, they have moved away from the don't-speak-with-each-other pressure imposed on Trump by the Russiagate coup plotters against him. This impasse is now broken. There was good chemistry between them, as reported by both sides. Both presidents clearly appreciate the fact that they represent large countries and feel responsible to their own countries first. However, they also know that their dialogue is, as I said, of uppermost importance for world peace.

So, given the fact that there was such a huge effort to prevent the summit from happening, it does represent an enormous breakthrough. What we do know about what was agreed upon at the meeting, is of truly extreme importance. They decided to set up four continuing joint working groups—one on economics for business leaders from both countries to meet to discuss proposals for successful business cooperation; one on military and anti-terrorism issues; one will be an expert council of political scientists, prominent diplomats and former military experts to look for points of contact between the countries to move the dialogue and interaction forward; and one on cyber-space—the two National Security Councils have already started meeting.

Now, the joint working group on cyber-security is the most interesting one, because it once again shows that Putin is an incredible strategist.

Investigative Report: On The Trail Of The 12 Indicted Russian Intelligence Officers

Michael McFaul, former Ambassador of the U.S. to Russia.

CC/Rod Searcey

While U.S. Special Counsel Robert Mueller (or "Muller" as he likes to call himself) decided at the last minute to make another desperado operation, by charging 12 Russian military officials of having meddled in the U.S. 2016 elections—a last-ditch effort to sabotage the atmosphere of the summit, Putin made a very smart offer, inviting Mr. Mueller to come to Russia to investigate these 12 individuals.

Putin's proposal is absolutely brilliant. Mueller probably thought that he would never have to produce any evidence, assuming that the Russians being charged, living in Russia, wouldn't come to the United States; there would never be a trial on the alleged evidence. Putin's inviting Mueller, himself, to come to Russia and investigate and interview people is a very brilliant move. Should Mueller refuse, he will really look bad. Putin reciprocally proposed that Russian specialists be permitted to go to the United States to interview former U.S. Ambassador to Russia, Michael McFaul, and Bill Browder, a crooked investor, who Putin says swindled the Russian state out of $1.5 billion in tax money. Interestingly, Christopher Steele is related to the Browder case, the Ukraine story, and Russiagate.

The White House has confirmed that Putin's proposal for such reciprocity was discussed between Putin and Trump. I think that this is probably the most brilliant outcome in the short term. Hopefully, in the long term, both countries will take up nuclear disarmament which their leaders discussed, while acting together to bring calm to the various hotspots around the world. It's also very good that Putin promised that he would support Trump in the American efforts to solve the North Korea crisis.

From our colleagues in America, I have received reports of tremendous positive response to the Trump-Putin summit. Many people are coming up to LaRouche PAC information tables saying, "I did not vote for Trump, but look at what he's doing—first, North Korea; now this summit with Putin. He's actually doing something very important."

Any sane person should be happy that the two largest nuclear powers, have indeed found a channel of communication at the highest level. If you contrast that accomplishment with the *insanity* of the media, and the loud-mouthed geopolitical politicians—one can only conclude that some of these people actually have deranged minds, not only the "Trump Derangement Syndrome." They are truly deranged; any person, who values world peace, should be happy about these developments. Remember that the U.S. military-industrial complex and its assorted hangers-on, need an enemy-image of Russia in order to keep their budgets intact.

This summit was really a breakthrough for civilization, and we should all be very happy about it.

Finally, Free Us From the British Empire

Schlanger: Leading into the summit, President Trump said repeatedly that neither Russia nor the United States would want to get into an arms race, and that preventing this is something that should be discussed. He also specifically talked about cooperation in Syria between the militaries of Russia and the United States.

What are the people who are attacking this doing? They're saying we need confrontation, whereas Trump said he would prefer diplomacy to confrontation.

Helga, this is all happening with the backdrop of the Mueller case. You mentioned the indictment of the 12 Russians before the summit, to try and break it apart. To go back a step, there was tremendous concern from the NATO countries that Trump was going to do something that would harm the U.S.-NATO relationship. You talked about ending the era of geopolitics. I think it's worth a second to look at what the geopoliticians are most afraid of, about what Trump is doing. Coming out of this summit, are we seeing the beginning of the end of the era of geopolitics?

Zepp-LaRouche: It's an important step in that direction. Look at the media response to this summit, and make a list of those media personalities who are screaming the loudest. Remember their names, because I can say with close to 100% certainty that at the next such occasion, it will be these same people who will try to manipulate public opinion again. It's actually useful to look at it this way: look at the public agents of what we call the British Empire, called by some in the United States, the Deep State—but that description is inadequate because it leaves out the British Empire direction, and outlook, of this mafia.

Since 1997, at least, my husband Lyndon LaRouche has said that in order to break the control of what we call the British Empire—which is not identical with Great Britain, it is the City of London/Wall Street control of the international financial institutions and also the elements of the military apparatus in cahoots with these interests—you need a great power alliance, including the United States, Russia, and China, and hopefully also India. Then you can add other countries to it.

However, you do need these large nations, which are economically, and militarily the strongest ones, and also the most populous, in order to define a New Paradigm, a new set of international relations. While we are still very far away from that new great power alliance, China has in fact created the New Silk Road dynamic, deliberately, explicitly based on the idea of respect for national sovereignty, respect for different social systems, and the principle of non-interference.

More and more countries are joining with the New Silk Road perspective, which includes importantly, the very deep strategic partnership between Russia and China. It is noteworthy that both Trump and Putin at the Helsinki summit talked about their "mutual good friend Xi Jinping." And it's also very important that China welcomed this summit, saying that it greatly contributes to saving world peace and bringing the world into order.

I think we should not be exuberant, however, because this is just a first step, and there are still insane reactions coming from inside the United States, from Democrats and also from some Republicans. One Democrat Congressman from Tennessee, Steve Cohen, went so far as to demand a military coup against Trump! These people are absolutely out of their minds. Some House Democrats began demanding that Trump's translator testify publicly in Congress on what the two Presidents discussed in their private one-on-one. This is really a high degree of hysteria. We also have Sen. John McCain and other people talking about "treason."

The treason being committed is, however, from those who are pushing for war! All such people are willing to risk nuclear war and the extinction of civilization, rather than have good relations between the United States and Russia. The big question here is who is actually committing treason?

It's interested that Putin commented on those criticizing the summit, saying that there are some people who, for their petty party politics, are risking the big issue of war and peace. They should really be ashamed of themselves—I'm saying that; I'm not quoting Putin.

So, it is an important step. The world is in a very rapid strategic realignment, with man nations including India, Japan, and most African nations and Latin American nations being part of this realignment. It is a good directionality. A lot will depend on getting to the bottom of Russiagate. If the United States and Russia are willing work together to investigate that, which they're now set to do with this committee on cyber-security, I think the danger can be eliminated. That cooperation between Russia and the United States will be an important step.

Schlanger: You mentioned earlier that we're getting readings that from the United States that many people actually feel liberated that Trump did this. From the radio interviews I do, I can report, that there's a tremendously positive response to Trump having the courage to go ahead with this meeting—in spite of Russiagate, in spite Mueller's grandstanding with 12 indictments of Russians right beforehand. Many people really see this just concluded summit as an opportunity to finally defeat the British Empire forces that have run

the post-Cold War order and now put us on the verge of a new hot war.

I want to bring up something you were just discussing: China. We have just produced a new, extremely important and timely report. The approach taken and the developments discussed in that report really constitute the alternative to the war policy of the Bush and Obama regimes; this is what Trump has to go towards: the Eurasian Land-Bridge. I'd like you to say a little bit about this new report.

Closer Africa-China Partnership

Zepp-LaRouche: As some of our viewers may know, we published the first World Land-Bridge report in 2014 under the title *The New Silk Road Becomes the World Land-Bridge*. That report found quite a resonance in the world; it was translated into Chinese immediately by Chinese institutions and was distributed widely to teaching faculties and think tanks. Then it was translated into Arabic and German.

In November 2017, the Schiller Institute published a Special Report, *Extending the New Silk Road to West Asia and Africa: A Vision of an Economic Renaissance*.

Now the Schiller Institute has released an expanded and updated 2018 report *The New Silk Road Becomes the World Land-Bridge: A Shared Future for Humanity, Volume II*. Taken together, these reports constitute a comprehensive blueprint for development in Africa, in building the economies of Southwest Asia, and also the Eurasian connections, as well as important projects in the United States and Ibero-America. These reports are absolute must-reads for anyone developing an interest in the New Silk Road and who wants to recognize the tremendous potential for all economies in the world to prosper.

One big feature is Africa, on which today there is a great focus because of the refugee crisis, but also because there is in Africa right now a tremendous potential for economic development. China's President Xi Jinping just started a trip which will take him to Senegal, Rwanda, Mauritius and South Africa. South Africa is the host of the 10th Annual BRICS summit, which will take place July 25-27. Xi's tour is expected to lead to a total

Xi Jinping, President of China (center foreground), with his wife Peng Liyun (behind him) and Macky Sall, President of Senegal (right foreground), with his wife Marieme Faye Sall (behind Xi's right shoulder) in Dakar, Senegal on July 22, 2018.

upgrade in Chinese investments and cooperation between China and Africa, already at an excellent stage.

In September, there will be a summit meeting of the Forum on China-Africa Cooperation (FOCAC) in Beijing of African leaders, which is expected to define a completely new level of cooperation and partnership between Africa and China.

We in the Schiller Institute are engaged in a campaign—we've discussed this already in some previous webcasts—to have the "Singapore model" applied to Africa, by getting the leaders of European and African nations, and hopefully also Xi Jinping, together in a summit that would announce a crash program for the infrastructure development of Africa. That was the subject of our June 30-July 1 conference, and I really urge all of you not only to buy a copy of this World Land-Bridge report Volume Two, which is an absolute eye-opener for anybody who wants to look into the future, the possibilities for development; but I also urge you, in case you haven't done it yet, to please watch the all the speeches from this conference in their totality.

The real difference and

Giuseppe Conte, Italian Prime Minister.

therefore significance of this conference, is that instead of just an analysis of particular problems, we discussed solutions. The conference participants also engaged in very important discussion about Southwest Asia and Africa, and about the reestablishment of international law. Many people recognize that we are in urgent need of going back to an idea of international law which is focussed on the general welfare of the people of the world, because the "survival of the fittest" idea of law has dominated the world in the recent decades.

This is all very important material. If you agree with our approach, you should become a member of the Schiller Institute. The Schiller Institute is a membership organization, because we want to create a Renaissance, and to do that, many people need to be engaged in sharing and distributing these positive views and development ideas.

Hysteria and Possibly War

Schlanger: Helga, one of the things that people are wondering about in the United States, is, in the aftermath of the NATO summit, which was quite frictional, what's the response in Europe to the Trump-Putin summit? Do you have much on that?

Zepp-LaRouche: Well, it's quite mixed. There was a very positive reaction from Italy. Prime Minister Giuseppe Conte welcomed the summit; Salvini, the Interior Minister, and head of the Lega party, invited Putin and Trump to hold their next summit in Italy. His comment about the summit was "Well done, well done, Presidents." Conte will also meet with Trump soon, and will also go to Moscow, so the diplomacy is very active.

Other reactions were much much worse. The German Foreign Minister mocked the summit. People with that type of attitude are so stuck in their geopolitical, backward looking, always-in-yesterday mode, that they are totally unable to have any vision for the future. Trump did attack the EU, calling it a "foe." Everybody in Europe was completely freaked out about that. The German proverb, "When you shout into the woods, it shouts back," well describes the effect being experienced by Europe's geopolitical elite. Look at the hysterical reactions of these Europeans from the first hour of Trump's election victory, they called him the most derogatory names you can imagine. I'm not surprised that Trump doesn't have a high opinion of these people.

On the other hand, a very measured response has come from some former diplomats who have said that it's good that these two largest nuclear powers are talking to each other. One former German ambassador said, "Europe should think more about its independence in its own way." I'm not against that all I think the policies of Brussels and Berlin depend not so much on Washington, because the moment Trump became President it became clear that it's not Washington as such that they feel subject to, but it is the British Empire. And I think if there is more independence from that, so be it. The New Paradigm is already on the horizon.

The best way to overcome the present tension would be to welcome the cooperation among the United States, China and Russia, and become part of that! There is a higher level of reason, where you can solve these problems, and I think the world needs to urgently move with a completely different way of thinking, what I call the New Paradigm. And for sure, overcome geopolitics, because geopolitics is what led to two world wars. If you don't get rid of geopolitical way of thinking, the danger exists of the extinction of civilization. For example, Paul Craig Roberts is very pessimistic. While he welcomed the summit, by looking at Trump's opposition, he predicts that there will be a war as a result of it. And if these voices have their say, Roberts may not be mistaken.

A very interesting comment came from a column in Lang's blog, *Sic Semper Tyrannis*, by someone writing under the pseudonym Publius Tacitus. I really would like people to read it, he says that those in the United States who are quick to blame Putin and Russia for everything should be aware that the United States has a history of intervening in other countries and ousting elected leaders—under previous administrations—and so the anti-Trumpers are sitting in the biggest glass house of all.

Such commentaries are extremely important and should be shared widely to counter the absolutely disgusting, mainstream "presstitutes," as Paul Craig Rob-erts likes to call them—a very appropriate name for people who are really, really doing a disfavor to their nation and to humanity as a whole. We should outflank them rather than pay attention to lying journalists who are provocateurs.

Wipe Out Speculation, Create National Banks

Schlanger: One relatively influential person that I speak with told me after the summit: "I'm sure this summit makes Lyndon and Helga very happy, because of their life's work oriented toward the Four Power agreement." And then he had a question for you. He said that he's heard you talk recently about the reestablishment of the Bretton Woods system, or a New Bretton Woods system. He said he researched this, and he saw that Lyndon LaRouche was putting this forward in the 1980s. He asked me to ask you: "How would a New Bretton Woods system work, and does it require active support from Russia, China, and the United States? Would that be enough to implement it?"

Zepp-LaRouche: The germ form of such a system already exists, in the e financial institutions associated with the New Silk Road: the Asian Infrastructure Investment Bank; the Silk Road Fund, the Maritime Silk Road Fund, the New Development Bank of the BRICS and many similar institutions including the emerging Africa investment fund. There you have regional institutions which already are lending for the real economy, rather than for speculation.

China is in the process of curbing speculation altogether. There has been a drop in international investment on the part of the Chinese, but that is mainly due to the fact that China is now outlawing speculative investments abroad. There are some countries that are already doing the right things, but obviously, the big, dark cloud on the horizon is the condition of the Western financial system, which is in terrible shape; for example, Deutsche Bank, with its Level 3 derivatives. There is a big worry about the future of the euro because of the so-called Target 2. Some people argue that this is all money which is irretrievable for some countries. There are many storm clouds on the horizon, notably the corporate debt bubble.

We will need some type of debt conference to get rid of the derivatives—Level 3 derivatives for sure, but also to untangle the speculative aspect, and then completely wipe out the speculative holdings. We can then establish institutions to create a credit system, with na-

Deutsche Bank is teetering. Deutsche Bank twin towers shown here.

tional banks in each country, and fixed exchange-rates among the currencies, perhaps with a gold reserve standard. Then the world would have a stable financial governance China has been calling for.

There has been no such set of proposals coming from Europe or the United States, but again, Italy may be an important factor in triggering such a discussion. Italy is the third-largest economy in Europe, and several ministers, and deputy or assistant ministers, have called for Glass-Steagall and a National Bank.

These are only steps in the right direction. The best thing that could happen would be that President Trump carries out his election campaign promise, namely, to implement Glass-Steagall, to go back to the American System of economy, and then reach out to the other countries to establish some kind of New Bretton Woods agreement. Such a happy action is not to be excluded, because he has a good record of bringing about his election promises.

So, if each country would set up a National Bank and its own credit system, clearing houses could be set up to discuss and negotiate long-term, international investment among the countries. It would be the responsibility of such clearing houses to seek equitable arrangements among the countries, considering their many differences: large countries with lots of raw materials and few people, like Russia; countries with small territory, relatively densely populated, with high-level industry, like Germany, Switzerland, Belgium; and small countries with few people and little industry. But all of these countries should somehow be part and partners of such a New Bretton Woods agreement, and that can be set up pretty much according to the model of the old Bretton Woods system.

I think this is definitely a discussion which should be held on an international level. One of the really big, threatening problems, still rumbling, is the potential of a disorderly financial collapse. That threat must be countered, by setting up a new financial architecture. With the New Silk Road, with the Belt and Road Initiative, there already exists the framework of the kind of model of cooperation among nations which is needed.

That is why we in the Schiller Institute are making such an effort to convince people of the benefits for every country participating in the New Paradigm, because that would really be the best way to have an orderly transition into a new set of international relations. And that is not an option. I think this is an absolute must, if we want to avoid chaos. Out of chaos there is always the danger of war, so this discussion is very timely and very urgent.

Schlanger: Imagine the reaction of the opponents of Trump, were Trump to do such a thing. The same people who today are arguing for war rather than diplomacy, would argue for the collection of their unsustainable debts, even to the extent of killing people, rather than taking the risk of writing down or writing off debt that never will be collected.

Helga, we've covered a lot, but I want to make sure that if there's anything else you want to bring up, you have the option to do so.

Find Out What Is Happening in Africa!
Zepp-LaRouche: I can only really invite you, once again, to join with us, because it *is* absolutely possible to reach a new era of civilization in the short term. I think you will agree with me that dramatic changes have taken place since the New Silk Road has been on the agenda, which is less than five years. A completely new optimism has emerged in Africa as a result of the New Silk Road policy. A new spirit has given Africans a completely new sense of self-confidence, that they can make the transformation into industrial countries, that they can create large middle classes, overcoming poverty and underdevelopment, building infrastructure, being partners for investment on an equal level with other countries of the West or of Asia.

America is very far away from Africa; admittedly Africa is closer to Europe than to the United States, but

I just can't believe that what is going on in Africa cannot but excite you, provided you know about it, which you won't if you confine your reading to the *New York Times*, *Washington Post*, or similar fare. *But it is happening!* I cannot believe that these potentials and developments carry no influence, or nothing exciting for, let's say, African Americans, and Africans in other countries as well, to really start to develop an active relationship between Africa, and the United States. Because I think that all of these questions—how to get rid of the trade deficit; sanctions or no sanctions—well, it's now clear, even the Federal Reserve's Beige Book finds that the tariffs are hurting a lot of American industries and making consumer prices higher.

And I have advocated all along that the better way is to have joint investments in other countries or continents, like the African continent. If the African Americans would start to take a really active interest in the kind of revolutionary changes which are taking place in Africa right now, maybe that would inspire many, many people to have a similar discussion on how America could be part of it, because a lot of industrial capacity will be needed and a lot of know-how and financing, in order to accomplish what could become the next big flowering of civilization. There are many people who are already saying that Africa will be "the next China, with African characteristics."

That was just an idea I wanted to throw out, and if any of you would like to respond to me, please, I'm happy to receive your email and we should have a dialogue about this, because for me, this potential for African development is one of the most joyful and exciting things of the present time.

Schlanger: With that, I think our viewers have now been given their marching orders: Join the Schiller Institute! Become engaged in a dialogue with us, but take that dialogue out to everyone. People all around the world are in revolt, they're in an insurgent state of mind. They want change, but they need to know what change means, and what change will work.

And so with that, Helga, thanks again, and we'll see you next week.

Zepp-LaRouche: Yes, until next week.

You're Human! Do You Know What That Means?

by Robert Ingraham

V.—Oligarchy

July 18—What is it that holds us back? What saps our moral commitment to build a better future? What force inserts the voice of pessimism into our minds that tells us that the only possible approach to our life is to "live for today" and make the best of a bad situation?

In the previous installment of this report, we looked at the great contributions made to human advancement, over several millennia, from China. The breakthroughs were astounding. Yet, in Europe, for almost 2,000 years—until the dazzling intervention by Dante Alighieri and then the great leadership provided by Filippo Brunelleschi and Nicholas of Cusa—the advancement of European culture was retarded. Our potential for development was poisoned.

In this chapter, we shall look at the subject of Oligarchy and Empire. We shall discuss history, but this is not a classroom exercise. The evil which afflicted Europe in the centuries prior to the Florentine Renaissance is with us, still, today. We see it in the financial policies of the City of London and Wall Street. We see it in the hostility to scientific advancement. And most of all, we see it in our culture; we see it within ourselves.

How many drug addicts are there, today, in America? How many alcoholics? How many victims of a perverse "pleasure and escapist" entertainment culture? Many good people try to close their eyes to the human devastation which surrounds them, much as Saint Augustine once covered his eyes while witnessing the barbarities in the Roman Coliseum—but blinders do not work; the carnage of this culture enters the lives of each of us. The day-to-day reality of living within a society that is destroying itself produces a numbing despair, and this eats away at the hope and courage within everyone.

Oligarchical power still exists, and oligarchic culture predominates. *This is our enemy. It is mankind's ancient and present enemy, and if you do not recognize the nature of your enemy, you can never hope to win.*

Recognizing the Enemy

We do not simply have a bad and corrupt culture in today's trans-Atlantic world. We live within an *oligarchic* culture, an *imperial* culture. It is a culture which tells you every day that you are not human, that you are impotent, that you have no power to affect the future. The policies of London and Wall Street—from geopoli-

The British Empire imposed the plague of opium on China by force of arms in its Opium Wars (1839-1842, 1856-1860).

tics to monetary speculation to the economic looting of the population—ensure that there is no basis for hope, or for a better future, within our society. We are rats in a maze, simply trying to make do.

This is not a natural state of affairs; it is not a human state of affairs! Rather, the true human condition is seen in what was earlier reported on the scientific advances in China, and the true human identity may be seen in the personality of Beethoven, or Louis Pasteur, or Alexander Hamilton. *Ours is a creative species, but this is what oligarchy has attempted to eradicate from our culture.*

If one wants to give a name to the "species character" of the oligarchical outlook, perhaps an apt choice would be *Malthusian.* Parson Thomas Malthus was both a pitiful figure and a plagiarist, but in his much-trumpeted work, *An Essay on the Principle of Population*, he puts forward an argument which defines the oligarchy's agenda, down to the present day. Malthus defines the human species as existing within an *entropic* biosphere, one governed by fixed laws and limited resources. He insists that humanity is subservient to these "laws of nature," and helpless to take command of its own future. He insists that any attempt by society to grow, to expand, will result in crisis and collapse. He justifies human suffering. This is an outlook which engenders deep pessimism within any person who accepts it.

In his demand that the human species be reduced in number, Malthus denies everything that is truthful about humanity. This is no accident, since Malthus was an agent of the British Empire, an empire then murdering millions all over the world. In the 20th century, an "updated" version of Malthus' argument was presented by H.G. Wells in his *Anticipations of the Reaction of Mechanical and Scientific Progress upon Human Life and Thought* (London, 1901), and Wells, together with that other "Typhoid Mary" of the British Empire, Bertrand Russell, devoted their lives

Rev. Thomas Malthus (1766-1834)

to eradicating the creative essence of the human identity from English-speaking culture.[1]

Beginning in the 1960s, through the launching of the British-created environmentalist movement, accompanied by the publication of such drivel as *The Population Bomb* (1968) and the *Limits to Growth* (1972), total war was declared on human culture. Mankind's creative nature—that which had inspired human progress since the discovery of the use of fire—was declared the enemy. Wells and Russell, together, denied the *noëtic* power of the human mind and demanded that human culture be reduced to the sensual appetites of a baboon or hyena. The current hegemonic acceptance of "environmentalism" within American and European societies is evidence of the success of their efforts.

You might think that all of this has nothing to do with you. But answer the following questions: Isn't there a limit on human population growth? Don't we need to conserve limited resources? Aren't we going to run out of fresh water? Isn't space exploration a waste of money? If you answered yes to any of them, you are infected with the oligarchical outlook, with a pessimism you don't even recognize. And it is that pessimism which leads to the drug epidemic we see today. It is precisely this pessimism which the oligarchy deliberately sows and fertilizes, because it is the best method for keeping the rest of us in self-imposed chains.

Roots

Oligarchism is a plague which is not new. It has infected our species since the time of the Bronze Age and the regimes of Sumer and Babylon. It is the system of imperial-oligarchical rule. In this installment of our report, we shall examine the murderous influence of oligarchical culture in modern European history. A

---

1. See "The Wells of Doom," Lyndon H. LaRouche Jr., *EIR*, Dec. 9, 1997.

Third Punic War, 149-146 BC. Rome obliterated the city of Carthage.

Julius Caesar (100-44 BC)

Oligarchic culture demands that you accept as fact that you are less than human. It denies—completely—the inherent creativity which has made possible all human progress. It drums this into our consciousness every minute of every day.

If you do not grasp the essence of what characterizes the oligarchic outlook, you will never learn how to defeat it, or how to be truly human.

Rome

If one traces the worst period of oligarchical rule in Rome—from the Third Punic War in 149 BC to the death of the last emperor in 476 AD—by that latter date, the total population of the Empire was lower than it had been 600 years earlier. To put it bluntly, that is all you really need to know to conclusively condemn the anti-human nature of Roman culture.[2]

Contrary to what almost everyone is taught in high school and university, the European "dark ages" did not take place in the centuries following the collapse of the Roman Empire. It was the Roman Empire, itself, which was the Dark Age. What followed its demise was merely the lawful devolutionary product of the devastation to human culture wrought by the 700-year rule of that imperial monstrosity.

Rome was an entropic society of zero-technological growth, built entirely on slave labor and economic looting. For six centuries there were no improvements in the methods of agriculture—from tillage, to fertilizer, to tools; no improvements in mining or metallurgy; no improvements in shipping and naviga-

comprehensive investigation is not possible within the constraints of this composition. Instead, we shall limit ourselves to certain characteristics of two case studies: the Roman and British empires.

We shall be discussing history, but the purpose of this is to make clear certain things about our current situation. Today, the most powerful elements of the trans-Atlantic financial empire are lashing out, attempting to destroy U.S. President Donald Trump, provoke confrontation with Russia and China, and sabotage the economic development policies of the Belt and Road Initiative. This financial oligarchy is the successor, the descendant, of the ancient empires discussed in this report, and the oligarchs of today are motivated by the same oligarchical outlook as their ancient predecessors.

Lyndon LaRouche has defined the enemy of humanity as the "Oligarchical Principle." It is of utmost importance that each of us thinks through the actual nature of this deadly oligarchic disease. An oligarchic system is an anti-human system. It denies human creativity. It is an *entropic* system—in direct opposition to the creative, self-developing nature of the universe.

---

2. None of what is said here should be taken to mean that human creativity ever vanished entirely under imperial rule, or that human beings ceased to be human beings. The great Cicero and Archimedes are exemplary of what is possible under even the worst conditions. Human creativity can never be extinguished. However, to appreciate the evil of oligarchy, keep in mind that Cicero, Archimedes, and Socrates were all murdered by their imperial rulers, as were Jesus Christ and Paul of Tarsus.

tion. Even previously known technologies such as water wheels and water pumps were hardly used, considered "more expensive" than the use of slave labor. Human productivity went backward, and true scientific investigation ceased to exist. Contrast this to what has been reported in earlier chapters of this report as to the pre-Roman breakthroughs in science, astronomy, engineering and navigation.

The initial expansion of the Roman Empire was carried out through genocide and enslavement. Julius Caesar, in fewer than ten years in Gaul, exterminated over 800 villages and sold over 1 million captives into slavery. After 117 AD, Rome stopped expanding geographically, and "internal" looting replaced foreign conquest, first among the far-flung Roman provinces and then against the people of Italy. This growing impoverishment and de facto enslavement of the Roman citizenry intensified over time, particularly during what historians like to call the "good" Antonine period.

This is precisely the "internal dynamic" of all imperial systems, down to the present day trans-Atlantic monetary empire. Human beings are mere commodities, and their labor is to be looted, through a variety of methods, to serve the interests of the oligarchical Leviathan.

As for monetary and financial policy, the historian Abbott Payson Usher has demonstrated[3] that what is usually considered to be the "modern" form of imperial global finance did not have its origins in London, Amsterdam, or even Venice, but that all of the later 13th, through 18th century "financial innovations" in those locations had their legal and political roots in the "concept of debt," as it was understood in the axioms of Roman and Byzantine Law.

Under Roman rule, progress stopped, science stopped, and the population was driven downward into a bestialized culture of "bread and circuses."

The Reckoning

From no later than 165 AD, continuing for three centuries, the Roman Empire was devastated by an on-

The Antonine Plague (165-180 AD) was brought home by Roman troops returning from the wars.

going series of epidemics and plagues, which never let up. During this entire period, the economic looting of the population together with ongoing military warfare (now almost entirely defensive) continued—and intensified—unabated.

Two of these epidemics, the Antonine Plague and the Plague of Cyprian, are often referred to as "great plagues,"[4] but, in addition to these, wave after wave of disease struck the empire for more than two centuries. It is suspected that the two "great plagues" were both smallpox, but it is also known that the continual series of epidemics included malaria, gonorrhea, leprosy, and measles.

The *Antonine Plague struck in 165 AD, and the first wave of the epidemic killed 4 to 7 million people throughout Europe*. During a second wave nine years later, reportedly 2,000 people a day were dying in the city of Rome. By 180 AD, it is estimated that somewhere between 25 to 50 percent of the entire population of the empire had perished.

The Plague of Cyprian raged from 250 to 270 AD. Sources from the period report that at the peak of the epidemic, 5,000 people a day were dying in Rome. During an outbreak in Carthage, a local deacon named

---

3. *The Early History of Deposit Banking in Mediterranean Europe.* See bibliography.

4. Prior to the 20th Century, the term "plague" was used generically to denote any devastating epidemic which killed large numbers of people, and its usage is not synonymous with what is now called the bubonic plague.

Pontius wrote of the disease:

> There broke out a dreadful plague, and excessive destruction of a hateful disease invaded every house in succession of the trembling populace, carrying off day by day with abrupt attack numberless people ... All were shuddering, fleeing, shunning the contagion, impiously exposing their own friends, as if with the exclusion of the person who was sure to die of the plague, one could exclude death itself also. There lay about the meanwhile, over the whole city, no longer bodies, but the carcasses of many ...

Rome's Oligarchical Twin

This same dynamic which devastated the Roman Empire in the west, also dominated the existence of its eastern sibling. What can one say about the Byzantine Empire? The zombie that refused to die? Byzantium was a parody of the Rome of Claudius, utilizing the same Roman methods of military conquest and economic looting. The tax farming and related monetary policies of Rome were brought in lock, stock and barrel. Under Byzantine rule, agricultural mills were abandoned, roads fell into disrepair, and local industries disappeared. In many areas water became scarce, as infrastructure collapsed. Whole sections of previously urbanized territory became ruralized or simply returned to wilderness. It was an empire based—in its entirety—on monetary wealth.

In 533 AD, the Emperor Justinian decided that he was going to reconquer the western Mediterranean and recreate the Roman Empire. Eight years into the war, one of the worst epidemics in human history struck Constantinople. The first wave of the epidemic lasted from 541 to 549 AD, spreading throughout Europe after the second year. In the capital, the peak of the epidemic lasted some four months and the death toll rose to a staggering 10,000 a day; more than 200,000 people were said to have died in Constantinople in the first year alone. By the time Justinian's plague had run its course, it had killed at least half the population of Europe, brought trade to a halt, and destroyed the empire. As one commentator said, "It then seemed to spread all over the [known] world; this catastrophe was so overwhelming that the human race appeared close to annihilation."

Mass Death

At this point, the effects of imperial/oligarchic rule are best stated by simply citing some statistics. The figures are obviously inexact, but the author has attempted to cross-check them with several sources. As already stated, the population of the Roman Empire was lower in 476 AD than it had been in 169 BC. As that Empire collapsed into chaos, the population of Western and Central Europe declined further:

Year	Population
350 AD	23 million
600 AD	13 million
780 AD	7 million

For the eastern Byzantine Empire, it looks like this:

Year	Population
350 AD	18 to 26 million
600 AD	10 to 16 million
780 AD	7 million

Then there are the effects of the Venetian-Mongol alliance of the 13th and 14th Centuries (a story which will not be told in depth here):[5]

Population of Europe (under Venetian monetary domination):

Year	Population
1200 AD	59 million[5]
1300 AD	78 million
1400 AD	39 million
1430 AD	22 to 24 million

Population of China (under Mongol Rule):

Year	Population
1200 AD	123 million
1400 AD	60 million

These figures are only shocking if one fails to grasp the *necessity* of continued human breakthroughs in science and technology for the survival and advancement of the human species. Human *discovery*, human *creativity*, and an anti-entropic increase in human *productivity* are all necessary features of human culture, without which the destruction of our species is fore-ordained. The toleration of imperial financial systems and oligarchical culture ensures a dy-

---

5. The increase in European population, between 780 AD and 1200 AD, was largely the result of the continuing effects of the reign of Charlemagne, as well as the introduction of new technologies which greatly boosted Europe's productivity, many of which entered Europe from China and the Abbasid Caliphate. This was also the era of what climatologists call the Medieval Warm Period, which had a very beneficial impact on European agriculture.

namic of collapse and extinction of human society. There is no possibility of a bucolic zero-growth human society. *Mankind either increases its productive power within the universe, through the social application of continual individual human discovery, or we die as a species.*

The Self-Imposed Entropy of Empire

The genocidal consequences of imperial policies of tax-farming, slavery, usury, and what Marxists would call "primitive accumulation" are self-evident. Their effects destroyed the Roman Empire, as well as the later Venetian trans-Alpine system of usurious banking in the 14th Century. These are the same policies which have characterized the entire history of the British Empire. At the same time, imperial rule has left humanity vulnerable to precisely the type of "galactic threats" which resulted in the extinction of many other species. We have touched upon some of this is Part Two of this series. Here, let us look deeper into the question of epidemic disease.

The historical record is clear that the looting policies of monetary empire exposes a weakened population to the ravages of disease. In the relevant case studies cited above, as well as in others, we see empires seemingly at the height of their "glory"—e.g., Athens under Pericles or the Rome of Marcus Aurelius—felled by epidemic disease. What characterizes all of these imperial systems is the ostentatious display of monetary wealth, while the population is driven downwards, and the truly creative arts of science and technology are diminished. All of these imperial systems exhibit a reduction in *per-capita energy consumption* and a decline in *potential relative population density*.

During the heyday of the Venetian monetary empire, starvation, warfare, and disease killed off 50 to 60 percent of the human beings in Europe. Some areas lost 80 percent or more. Including the death toll from Venice's partner, the Mongol Empire, and folding in the rest of the Mediterranean region, the final number of human corpses had to have been in excess of 100 million. Some sources claim that in the period from 1276 to 1350, life expectancy in Western Europe dropped from 35 years to 17 years. Parts of Asia and Europe, today, still have lower population densities than in 1250 AD. Most of France and Italy did not return to those earlier population levels until the 19th Century, and for much of southwest Asia and northern Africa this did not happen until the 20th Century.

The Cosmos and Disease

Several of the worst disease pandemics in human history (in the 3rd, 6th, and 14th Centuries) were preceded by violent shifts in weather patterns and climate, patterns largely determined by an array of galactic influences.

Take the case of the 14th Century Black Death. The "Medieval Warm Period" ended abruptly in 1314 with the onset of brutally cold and incessantly wet weather. This was the preliminary phase of the "Little Ice Age," which would continue for centuries, bringing even much colder weather by the 17th Century. By 1315, there were universal crop failures. People died of starvation on a massive scale. There was no corn, no bread, no anything, and hunger was universal. Diseases such as pneumonia, bronchitis, typhoid fever, dysentery, diphtheria, and tuberculosis finished off many of the weakened population who did not starve outright.

All across Europe most of the livestock died, either from starvation, or from the accompanying spread of epidemic diseases such as rinderpest. By the time it was all over in 1322, somewhere between 10 and 20 percent of the population of Europe north of the Alps, were dead and the region was a wasteland. Then, in 1347 the Black Death struck the already devastated population.

Throughout this entire period, the Venetian monetary empire, and its Lombard and Angevin allies, intensified their tax-farming, debt usury, and other forms of financial looting—all reminiscent of the earlier practices of Rome. The population of Europe was driven downward, industry and agriculture collapsed, and the ability to defend against disease and climate change evaporated. *This is how species go extinct.*

The British Empire

The modern oligarchical spawn of these ancient imperial systems is the British Empire, which is with us still today. Through its banking and monetary power, as well as the multifaceted control it maintains over global narcotics trafficking, news media, entertainment, food cartels, armies and political institutions in the trans-Atlantic world, it is the paramount enemy of mankind.

This is precisely the empire which is presently mobilized to destroy the efforts by Donald Trump, Vladimir Putin and Xi Jinping to implement a grand strategy of peace through economic development.

The public record of British genocide, far worse than Adolph Hitler, is readily available. Those who deny such evidence suffer from a mental affliction. The British Empire was the leading slave trader, narcotics trader and author of mass murder for centuries. And there is nothing to indicate that they have changed; they simply no longer possess the unchallengeable global hegemony to rule unchecked.

The question arises: "Are the British oligarchs actually human?" In perhaps the only truthful utterance which ever passed from her lips, Queen Victoria once referred to her progeny as "frog-like," and were it not for the recent practice by European royalty to procreate with "commoners," it could be argued that the modern Olympian aristocracy has been self-degenerating—reverting biologically—to a lower animal species. Certainly, a history of mental afflictions, not to mention

Queen Victoria (1819-1901)

hideous physical features and other congenital defects, have plagued generations of that inbreeding class.

The semi-incestuous family members of the oligarchy exhibit all of the characteristics of a lower-ordered species, or of a renegade branch of the *Homo* genus, who upon seeing the first human-lit fire fled back to the jungle. Thus, the World Wildlife Fund is aptly named, for it captures the essence of their species-identity.

Isn't this what they are? Adam Smith and his "pursuit of pleasure and avoidance of pain"? Humanity would have suffered extinction long ago if it had followed that dictum. All of modern British "science" and philosophy has promoted a non-human concept of the human identity, and one which flies in the face of two million years of human acts of discovery. From Hume to Locke to Bertrand Russell, spokesmen of the empire have proclaimed, "We are not human," and maybe they aren't. But we are.

The history of the human species demonstrates that only the power of creation which exists within the human mind—a power coherent with the developing nature of the universe—will allow for human society to develop into the future. The oligarchical principle is anti-cognitive. It suffocates and murders precisely that creative identity which allows human culture to progress. This is why all empires disappear. They possess no means to thrive. The only question is how many of us they will kill before they go, or whether we kill oligarchy first.

Oligarchy does not simply impose its power on the population, like a bunch of storm-troopers or slave mongers. It gets us to enslave ourselves. This is the issue of culture. If we accept the idea that our primary base instinct is the "pursuit of pleasure and avoidance of pain," if we allow the pessimism of the oligarchical outlook to enter our hearts, we are already defeated.

An insight into the Satanic degeneracy of the British oligarchs who financed the rise of Adolph Hitler may be obtained through the viewing of the 1936 film *Ewiger Wald* (Eternal Forest). It is all there: the brutish worship of mother earth, the glorification of nature and "primaeval man,"—and Nazism as the pinnacle of that outlook.

To be continued.

February 14, 2004

I Stand At the Bedside of A Doomed Empire

by Lyndon H. LaRouche, Jr.

This is a transcription of the keynote address of Lyndon La-Rouche, to the annual Presidents' Day conference of the International Caucus of Labor Committees and Schiller Institute, Feb. 14, 2004.

This is, as I have promised, a truly momentous occasion. It's a historic occasion, more than historic. Because, we're looking at not only the collapse of an empire, which came into being about 250 years ago, between 1755 and 1763, when the British victory over the French, in particular, established the British East India Company as an empire, casting itself in the image of the Roman Empire, an empire which was constituted by a group of banking interests, essentially of Venetian origin, which ran the British East India Company, and ran the Company as, itself, an empire. At that point, in 1763, the British Empire, as it then existed, was led by a man who had not quite reached his 30th birthday, known as the Marquess of Lansdowne, later,

Wikimedia ccmmons

"The Death of the Miser" (detail) by Hieronymous Bosch.

Presidential candidate Lyndon LaRouche describes to a national conference the imminent death of that bankers' empire known today as the IMF/dollar financial system, and traces its history back to the British East India Company's and Lord Shelburne's assault against what the American Revolution represented.

EIRNS/Stuart Lewis

and also more notorious as Lord Shelburne. This man set forth two operations in place, which have governed the direction of world history—as world history—from that time to the present day. The first intent of Shelburne was to destroy the English-speaking colonies of North America. And he assigned a number of people, including Adam Smith, as agents, to conduct that policy.

This was a policy which led to the American Revolution, and led to the establishment of the greatest threat which the British Empire has faced, to the present day: the American Revolution, and the establishment in 1789, of the Federal Constitution of the United States. The greatest single threat to the empire, on this planet, over the entire past quarter-century has been that process, which created the United States.

At the same time, Shelburne and Co., through agents including Adam Smith, most notably Jeremy Bentham, and others, organized in France, around some of the followers of Voltaire, organized a cult, a freemasonic cult called the Martinists. This Martinist cult, which included assets of Shelburne, such as Jacques Necker of Lausanne, Switzerland, Philippe Égalite@ee, and others, set into motion on July 14, 1789, the Bastille event, which was intended to bring the danger of the spread of the influence of the United States to an end worldwide. Because, at that moment, you had had the attempt by Bailly and by Lafayette, to introduce a reform in France, which would have established a constitutional monarchy, which would have steered that monarchy along economic-development lines, akin to those policies adopted by the United States, with its Constitution.

So again, this is the way history has gone. The two English-speaking foci of the current of world history: the United States, which represented the best currents in Europe—typified by the Classical humanists and the influence of Leibniz; typified by the tradition of the Treaty of Westphalia; typified by the legacy of the 15th-Century Renaissance: These were the great English-speaking forces in the world, which were assembled for a collision, which is now coming to a point of historic decision, in the weeks and months immediately ahead of us.

One way or the other, this is the end of the Anglo-Dutch Liberal model of parliamentary government, and its influence in the United States—either for better, or for *very much worse*.

Policy Was To Crush the United States

Now, it should be recalled, that the Martinists, who were used by Shelburne, and run largely, directly out of London by Bentham, as the head of the secret committee of the British Foreign Office, which had been created by Shelburne: They ran the French Revolution. They ran the affair of the Bastille. They ran the Jacobin Terror. Danton and Marat were British agents, trained in London, deployed from London, and delivering speeches in France, *written in London*, under the direction of Bentham. The Jacobin Terror was *run from London*. Napoleon was a creation of the Martinist freemasonic lodge, the Napoleonic Empire. And then, when the time came, that Napoleon and his empire had essentially destroyed much of Europe, then the British said, "Okay, get rid of Napoleon." It was done by Germans, actually.

And they set up the Vienna Congress—which was a "sexual" Congress of Vienna, where countesses and others diverted the count-heads of state for the British, and Castlereagh and Castlereagh's stooge in Austria, ran what became the Vienna Congress.

And in good time, as the British had planned well, that Metternich disappeared, over the period from 1830-1832 to 1848. It was an operation run by Bentham's successor, Lord Palmerston, who ran Giuseppe Mazzini, the head of Young Europe, an organization which included Karl Marx. The entire operation of the Revolution of 1848, was run by British intelligence, for the purposes of finishing off the power of the Habsburgs, and making them a subordinate agent, within a British-controlled empire.

We were almost crushed, repeatedly. The intention of Britain was to destroy us. This was the perpetual policy, of the British toward the United States, and the policy of the key traitors within the United States: such as Gallatin, such as Aaron Burr, such as the leadership of many of the political parties. The controllers of agents, such as Andrew Jackson, Martin Van Buren, Polk, Pierce, Buchanan, who were agents of the enemy, determined to destroy us.

In the process, the American patriotic tradition had a resurgence, around the tradition of Lafayette, around the personality of John Quincy Adams, and with a very significant recruit by John Quincy Adams to his cause, the Whig, Abraham Lincoln, who was Quincy Adams' voice in the Congress, in denouncing the Polk Presidency for the war against Mexico, of that period. And that President Lincoln, later, led the United States to return to itself, as a nation. And we emerged from that Civil War, as the greatest single nation-state power on this planet, in terms of economics. The British had more power, as an empire, but, we were the most powerful state, the greatest economy, the most progressive economy, in the world, by 1876.

This was the work of Lincoln's revolution: We had become *ourselves*. But, meanwhile, the Anglo-Dutch Liberals were already at work, subverting us, with Andrew Johnson, who was a disaster, and others.

Corruption Sets In

And so, we went through these processes. At the beginning of the century, we were destroyed by the assassination of a President, McKinley. It was an assassination run by the same interests, for the purpose of putting Teddy Roosevelt in the Presidency. Teddy Roosevelt was a member of the Confederacy tradition: His uncle, who trained him, who steered him, who crafted his career, Bullock, was the chief of intelligence of the Confederacy, who operated from London during the period of the Civil War.

The real successor of Teddy Roosevelt—who destroyed the American System, in the name of "trust-busting"; he destroyed the American System, in order to create hegemony for New York-based, British and other bankers, for their system. In other words, he transferred the power, from industry and agriculture, to the financiers. He was succeeded, by a passionate advocate for the revival of the Ku Klux Klan: Woodrow Wilson. And Woodrow Wilson launched the mass mobilization and revival of the Ku Klux Klan, in the United States, during his Presidency, *from the White House*, publicly and personally.

So, this was the corruption which grabbed us, from the time of the McKinley assassination, until Franklin Roosevelt. And Franklin Roosevelt, *despite his own party*, became President. His party did everything possible—the Democratic Party—to *prevent* him from becoming the Democratic nominee! And, it was also the same filthy bankers, of the Teddy Roosevelt/Woodrow Wilson tradition who did it.

But, Franklin Roosevelt saved the United States, in a unique way, by his leadership. But then, he died. And even before he died, we were in trouble.

The history of this process in the 20th Century is quite interesting. The British policy, that is, the policy of the British East India Company, and its followers, had always been to use war on the continent of Europe, as a way of putting the nations of continental Europe against each other's throat, in such a fashion, there would never be a threat of a challenge to British supremacy, from the continent. This was a characteristic of the 19th Century. It was also the continuing characteristic, deep into the 20th Century.

So, time came, at the end of the so-called First World War, which had been concocted by the British, especially by a man who had been dead—Edward VII, the man who created the Federal Reserve System in the United States through his agents here, including Teddy Roosevelt and Woodrow Wilson. The British had decided at the end of World War I, to close in, and create a new kind of world empire. The empire was the empire of fascism: It was the empire of the Synarchist International, which we knew as fascism from 1922 through 1945. The forces behind this fascism, were bankers, including Lazard Frères, in France; and others. These bankers conspired to install fascism on the continent of Europe.

Some of these fascists went further, around Hitler. They conceived of creating a world empire, along the following lines, which came to a crisis point in 1940, when the remains of the British Expeditionary Force were sitting on the sands at Dunkirk, waiting for Hitler's tanks to pounce, and finish them off. Hitler held back his tanks, at that time—very momentous. Because, Hitler thought that the British Establishment was going to join the Nazis in a program of world conquest, whose included target was the destruction of the United States. Here was the plan. Now, this is Churchill, as Defense Minister of Britain, sitting in opposition to these fascists, not because he wasn't a fascist; but because he didn't think it was in British interests to play this game. Or, British imperial interests.

The fascist plan, including people in London of very high rank, some of whom were never prosecuted for what they did, conceived of taking the British Navy, the German Navy, the French Navy, the Italian Navy, and the Japanese Navy, as one force, which, once the Soviet Union had been quickly destroyed by this alliance, would then turn on the United States and destroy the power of the United States. The reason that didn't happen, is that the British Navy did not join the Nazis at that point, that Hitler was sitting there poised, ready to receive them with open arms, as part of his alliance—which is why he didn't crush the British Expeditionary Force, when he could, at Dunkirk.

Churchill said, "No, we will not let someone from the continent of Europe, even if we like his nastiness, such as Hitler, to take over control of the British Empah! And therefore, we will even degrade ourselves, to go to our so-called 'American cousins'—even to one we hate the most, Franklin Roosevelt—and seek his cooperation in defeating the Nazis." So, a German official, Canaris, who was not exactly a Hitler man, prevailed upon

NATO photo   EIRNS/Stuart Lewis

"If we can not change, if we select our choice of President, if we select our policies, now, in these weeks and months, the way things are going now, in general, this nation will not long survive."

Francisco Franco—another nasty fascist, in the tradition of the Inquisition—not to occupy Gibraltar: Because, had the alliance gone through, and had Gibraltar been occupied by the Nazis, i.e., Franco, then the Mediterranean would have been a closed lake, controlled by this alliance. Under those conditions, the existence of civilization would have been in jeopardy. Canaris prevailed upon, and frightened Franco, into refusing Hitler's demand that he seize Gibraltar.

So, this combination of decisions: Churchill says, the British fleet will go to Canada, if England is invaded, and will ally with the United States. This decision did not prevent the war, but it ended the possibility of Hitler's world conquest.

A Turn Toward Utopian Policies

Therefore, in 1944, once the Allied forces, led by the United States, had made the breakthrough in Normandy, and the Wehrmacht position on the continent of Europe was in terminal jeopardy—and was saved only because the British intelligence services informed the Nazis of the plot for peace, and they hanged the generals, in July 1944. At that point, there was turn in U.S. policy: that those bankers who had been for Hitler, like Harriman, Morgan, Mellon, du Pont—the same types of bankers who had conspired to assassinate the President of the United States in 1933-34, in the thing that was testified before the Congress on the Generals' Plot—these guys went back to their old ways.

Their policies were, at that point: Take a right turn; go to a utopian policy; use weapons of mass destruc-

tion, including the nuclear weapon which the United States was developing in experimental mode, at the time; and air power, to conduct a new kind of warfare. And to use a war against the Soviet Union, or with the Soviet Union, as the pretext for this policy. In other words, going back to the same Nazi policy that Hitler and Co., and his allies in France, in Italy, and so forth, had had up to June 1940: Go for a war against the Soviet Union, as the way of putting this policy into place.

We had, in the United States, we had a reign of terror in the United States which reached a peak, in about 1947. Later, it became known as McCarthyism. McCarthy was a joke—Joe McCarthy. Truman was the problem. But, not all of our people in this country were fools. There was the plan already, which I, sort of, was party to, in a, sense in 1947: to have Eisenhower run for the Democratic nomination, and get Truman out of there. The only way to save the United States. Eisenhower turned it down, but did run for President later.

Then, Truman got us into a Korean War, through his own stupidity, his own recklessness, his own fascist qualities. Some people may not like that, but that's what he was, don't kid yourself. He's a bankers' man.

And the Korean War became a mess. And, about the same time, it was discovered that the Soviet Union had developed priority in a thermonuclear, deployable weapon.

Preventive nuclear warfare, using air power, went off the agenda. Truman was told not to run again. Eisenhower was put in place. The Korea mess was put into—not deep freeze, but was put into some kind of management. And we stumbled through two Presidencies fairly well.

But then, when Eisenhower left office, warning against the danger, not in a clear way, but in a frank way—some honest details—warning against what he called "the military-industrial complex." The military-industrial complex was nothing other than the Bertrand Russell policy, the Winston Churchill policy, the policy of what we call the "Utopians" in the United States, of using nuclear weapons and air power, as a way of *terrorizing* the world into submitting to world government: a new form of empire; an echo of the Roman Empire; a continuation, in a new form, of the British Empire.

That's what he was warning against, when he said "military-industrial complex"; it was not a "military-industrial complex," it was actually a commitment, by the same crowd whose policies are expressed by Cheney, today, for world government, through nuclear terror.

We have lived under different, various phases of nuclear terror, since the close of the war. It was for this reason, that Truman dropped two totally unnecessary nuclear weapons on Japan, on the civilian populations of Hiroshima and Nagasaki. The last two weapons of the type we had—they were experimental prototypes. It took some time, before we got online, producing nuclear weapons in a line sense. So, we went first. Truman's policy was the policy of *preventive nuclear warfare!* The policy designed by Bertrand Russell, the man who's considered a pacifist. I guess killing everybody makes you a pacifist: Nobody shoots back.

That was the policy—until the Soviet development of a deployable, thermonuclear instrument was known. At that point, Bertrand Russell opened negotiations with Stalin's successor, Khrushchov. This was done in London. And, what happened was, that Khrushchov and Russell agreed on negotiating a system, a so-called permanent system of world rule, based on what we later called "Mutual and Assured Destruction."

Now, once Eisenhower was out of office, having made his warning speech, the right wing surged forward, in the form of Allen Dulles's caper, the Bay of Pigs. It surged forward, in the realization of the plan which Khrushchov and Russell, among others, had concocted, in the form of the 1962 Missile Crisis. And after the Kennedy assassination, which cleared the way for launching the Indo-China War, we underwent a great change, which leads to the immediate subject we have to consider *now, in these weeks*: We have to decide, as a nation, as nations, whether civilization will survive on this planet. That decision will be made, in the course of the coming weeks! And I shall indicate what the problem is. But first, get the situation.

Transformation in Our National Character

What happened was, that we, in the United States, underwent a transformation in our national character, which has threatened us with doom, today. The danger comes, not from someone outside our skins. It comes from our own people. It comes from those who are largely 60 years of age, or slightly younger: the so-called Baby-Boomer generation, which occupies the key positions in government, business, and other institutions of the United States, today. *This is the source of the danger.* Not someone from the outside, but a generation from the *inside*, which did what? They underwent a cultural paradigm-shift, as it's called, typified by the rock-drug-sex counterculture, during the middle of the 1960s. This was the result of the cumulative effect on their parents' generation—that is, my generation—and on themselves.

Remember, their parents' generation had gone through what? We had gone through a nightmare, the Coolidge-Hoover-Mellon nightmare. We were being destroyed as a nation. I can tell you, from my memory of the 1920s, *we were disgusting!* And then, we were hit by the Depression. And we became sheepish, frightened, worried.

Roosevelt appealed to the "forgotten man," in a campaign speech delivered in West Virginia. This aroused the nation. He was able to *defeat* the Democratic Party, and become the Presidential nominee. The nation was inspired, with the idea that recovery, that hope was possible.

People had been ground down, already. Their character, our character, changed in the beginning of the 20th Century. Look at the literature. Look at what was considered popular entertainment. Look at the popular culture, at the beginning of the 20th Century: It was disgusting! This is the period of Jim Crow! It was disgusting! We were a disgusting people, in our behavior. We were humiliated, like the hand of God had humiliated us! We were thrown into a Depression: "I guess we weren't so good, huh? We must'a made some mistakes, huh?"

But, not only were we humiliating, in our illusions, in our delusions: We were also given hope. We were given a chance, the reality of a recovery that this, too, shall pass. We were inspired. And this degree of inspiration continued in the American forces, in the United States and overseas, for example—the military forces—up until about the time the two bombs were dropped on Hiroshima and Nagasaki.

Things were going bad already. But, this *little man*—this Truman—. There was an incident I had, when I was in service in India, on my way into northern Burma. And, some GIs came to me—Roosevelt had just died; the announcement had just come through. They said, "We want to talk to you." (This was during the daytime.) "Can we meet tonight?" So, we had one of these improvised meetings at night, with a bunch of GIs and me. And the question was: What does the death of Roosevelt mean for us? My answer was simple. I said, "I don't know. But, I'm terribly worried, that such a great President should be replaced, in such a time as this, by this *terribly little man.*" And I was right. The right wing took over.

I saw people, who had been battle-hardened, who I though I had understood; and within a year or so, after returning from military service into civilian life, I saw people who had been turned into stinking cowards. This was my generation. This was 95% of my generation. It was later called "McCarthyism." It was actually better called "Trumanism," because it was done under Truman. And it was done under the Harriman crowd, the same Harriman crowd, who had been part of the forces that had *put Hitler into power in Germany in the first place*! The right wing had taken over America.

There was a reaction, a reaction against the Korean War. The Eisenhower reaction. There was a feeble attempt, around President Kennedy, to go back in the direction that we had been, under Roosevelt. That was crushed. Young people, whose parents had become prostitutes—i.e., my generation: "Don't say anything, don't do anything, don't think anything, that might get our family into trouble. Think of your father's job! Don't say anything. Don't associate with anybody who might get you in trouble, and jeopardize your father's job! Or cause you to be ostracized in your school, by a whispering campaign." Everybody was afraid of the FBI. The great scarecrow of America.

The children were raised: [whispering] "Be careful!"

"Be bold! Be optimistic! Be bright! Be shiny! Be acceptable! Learn to 'go along to get along!'"

"Go with the crowd. Go with the flow."

And the flow was civil rights. The flow was similar things. And these young people went along with it. They played a significant role in this. But then, they were hit by the hammer: the hammer of the Missile Crisis—where people were going into bars, looking for God. Atheists were suddenly jumping into a beer-keg— "I found God!" And, for several days, that was the characteristic of this country. I was there; I remember; I saw it! Don't tell me it didn't happen; I was there. I was a witness to it.

I saw most of entire generations go insane! My generation is, again, insane: Fear! Crumbled before the

EIRNS/Stuart Lewis

Lyndon LaRouche with civil rights heroine Amelia Boynton Robinson, vice president of the Schiller Institute. Her and LaRouche's appearance at a Talladega, Alabama commemoration of Martin Luther King Day on Jan. 19 is being discussed all over the country; the DVD of LaRouche's presentation, "The Immortality of Martin Luther King," is circulating in the thousands.

idea of an Indo-China War—*crumbled!* Everything they said they had fought for—no longer!

The Cult of Dionysus Takes Over

And their children had gone worse than crazy: the rock-drug-sex counterculture. Remember where it had occurred: The rock-drug-sex counterculture, which had existed as the "beatnik culture" of the early of 1950s, emerged where? It emerged among young people, in universities, either on state subsidies or families which could afford the tuition, at the leading Ivy League and other universities in the United States, presumably studying to master history, to master science, professions, and so forth. What are they doing? They're fleeing from their textbooks, into a night with marijuana, and red wine, mixed. A night with LSD. A night with sex with anything that crawled, and then figure out what the sex was in the morning. This was what happened! The throbbing beat of the drum: to silence thought, to silence *all* thought. Wild entertainment. The Cult of Dionysus, reborn in America.

Where did it start from? It started from the so-called "cream of the crop"—the young generation, entering universities, especially leading universities, during the middle of the 1960s. They turned against technology:

"Technology's bad! We've go to stop technology. We've got to go back to nature." And they took their clothes off, to prove it.

We became that. Therefore, we have undergone what is called a cultural paradigm-shift, over the past 40 years, in which the generation which entered universities in the middle of the 1960s, are the worst offenders. And the more high-ranking they are today, generally, the worse they are. Because, they represent the leading edge of a cultural trend. It's a great cultural transformation: *And this is the great source of danger.*

See, we've been through depressions, follies, before. But this has something different in it. We, in the United States, never before, as almost, virtually, an entire generation, have repudiated the culture of modern Western European civilization. And this, of course, spread in Europe the same way. It's spread in other parts of the world. We never repudiated it. We sinned against it, we violated it, but we didn't *repudiate* it! For 40 years, the generation now in leading, controlling positions of power in the United State, Europe, and elsewhere, have repudiated civilization.

A Corresponding Shift in Economic Policy

We have, in the United States, gone from being, in Kennedy's time, the world's leading producer society—the greatest producer of agricultural and industrial goods, the world leader in technology: We went from being that, to becoming a relic, a caricature of Rome under the Caesars.

Especially after 1971-72. In 1971-72, what did we do? We shut down the monetary system, the fixed-exchange-rate monetary system that Roosevelt had established. The system which had given us the possibility of recovery in the post-war period. We shut it down. We went to what is called a floating-exchange-rate system.

And, what did we do, with this floating-exchange-rate system? We went to poor countries of the world, more and more; we said, "*We* will determine the value of your currency, under a floating-rate system." We sent the IMF and the World Bank to enforce it. We pushed down the value of their currencies, by speculative runs, organized on the London financial market. We then went to the government, and said, "Call in the IMF. Call in the World Bank. Get some advice." The advice was, "Drop the value of your currency."

And the frightened governments said, "All right. So, we'll pay in our—"

"No!! You don't pay in your money any more! You pay in dollars!"

"How do we do that?"

"Well, we give you a debt, an additional debt, you didn't incur. We dictate it to you. We create it, and we tell you to take it. This debt is based on the estimated difference in value between your currency before we devalued it, and afterward."

That is what the debt of South and Central American countries, today, is. There's no country in South and Central America, in general, which owes a nickel to anybody! Including Argentina. The debt is entirely artificial. [applause]

Sucking the Blood of the World

And then, what did we do? And, look at Mexico, after 1982, after what they did to Mexico in 1982, between August and October of 1982. What did they do? They destroyed the Mexican economy! What did they do then? They said, "We will use your cheap labor."

So, what we have done, as a nation, we have gone to the poorest countries of the world—or those we made poor, by decree; we told them, "You will now produce cheap goods, for us! And they're going to be cheap, buddy—even if you die doing it!"

Then, we said: Okay. We're getting our goods, not from our production. We're getting it from cheap labor, in foreign countries. Therefore, we can shut down our factories. We can go into globalization. We can let NAFTA go into effect. *We now suck the blood of the world.* We bring slave labor into the United States, and we call it "illegal immigrants." But, we bring it in, because we want the cheap labor. We force Mexico to supply cheap labor, even at the cost of the *lives*, of people who are paid so little that they can not survive, or raise a family on that income, not physically. We do the same thing throughout South America.

We conduct genocide in Africa, because, in 1974, Kissinger and others devised a policy of genocide against Sub-Saharan Africa. The policy, "Those raw materials in the Africa—they belong to *us*! We can't let the Africans use them up. If we let their population grow, they will use them up! If we let Africans have technology, they will use them up more rapidly.

"Therefore, we have to do something about these Africans. And their voracious tendencies to survive.

"How do we do it? *Genocide*!"

And genocide is an Anglo-American-Israeli trick, in Africa. It's that simple. It's done through corporate vehicles, it's done in other ways; it's done through private

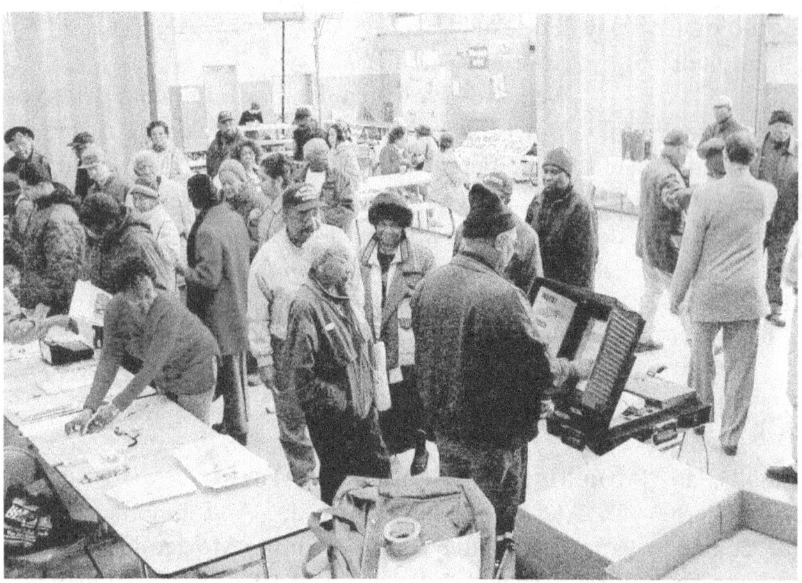

A Democratic caucus in Washington, D.C., Feb. 14, 2004, to select Democratic delegates. At LaRouche's keynote that day, his campaign spokeswoman Debra Hanania-Freeman reported that hundreds of LaRouche supporters were arriving at caucus sites in the nation's capital and being blocked from voting for LaRouche by the use of electronic "touch-screen" machines and other methods.

armies, organized in the usual, customary way. The same way Iran-Contra was organized. That's how it's done.

So, what we've done, is we've now created a world, which is no longer self-sustaining. Europe is bankrupt. It just happens that the United States is more bankrupt. And Japan, financially, is the most bankrupt nation in the world. How'd they become bankrupt? By subsidizing the United States' dollar.

So, we now come to a world, which, in terms of Europe and the Americas, can not survive on its present levels of productivity. Our level of infrastructure collapse, in the United States today, in power generation and distribution, in mass transit, and so forth, is poorer, by a large margin, than the time when Franklin Roosevelt was elected President. We are on the verge of destruction.

And what's the enemy?

A Sane Alternative

Well, what are the alternatives? As President of the United States, or if it were decided that I was going to be nominated, as President of the United States, today, the problem would be under control, as far as the international monetary-financial system exists. Because, I know, from our discussions with people in Europe, and elsewhere, that the potential—just like what happened yesterday, in Italy, in this discussion there, in the Italian Parliament: that the people in Europe, if the United States would make certain proffers of policy, that most of the nations of continental Europe—including many of the Brits—would agree to go along with that policy, which would be essentially, a return to the philosophical standpoint of the original Bretton Woods agreement, to put the entire present system into monetary-financial reorganization; to ensure stability, and to launch a pattern of growth on this planet.

That, in a sense, echoing what Roosevelt did, philosophically, in 1933-34, that can be done today. It requires the political will; it requires an initiative from a President of the United States, or someone who was understood as going to *be* a President of the United States. Under those conditions, leading nations of Europe and other parts of the world, will immediately begin to adapt to such a proposal from the United States. That, I can guarantee. My job is to deliver that. Because, I'm the only American who knows how to do it, and has the credibility around the world, to be believed, in doing that.

That's one side of the problem. But, why isn't that decision made? Why are Americans insane? Why don't Americans pick a President, whose role would ensure a solution, for a problem which is crushing the people of the United States, among others? Why are they so insane? Because we have gone—in the generation which dominates politics, which dominates life in the United States today—we have gone from being a producer society, whose standard of values is to measure things in terms of productive output, and producing for the needs of humanity, to a Roman-style pleasure society.

Look at the minds, look at the minds of the generation now in their fifties and early sixties. *Look at them!* What are their attitudes? And what is the conflict, which has emerged, in the United States, in particular, between young people who are over 18 years of age into the twenties, and their parents' generation? Studies have been made, by political institutions of the United States, over the recent period: Several years ago, there was a change, a fundamental change, in relationships between the youth generation and their parents' generation, from a sense of tolerant friction, to one of hostility. Young people today, in Europe, as in the United States, are saying to their parents' generation, "You have given us a no-future society, in which to live! You are the enemy. Not because you're the enemy, but because, as long as you insist, successfully, on imposing this no-future society on us, *we don't have a chance to live!* And you won't have any children or grand-children, to work for."

What has happened is, today, you have people who, as a result of the cultural paradigm-shift, no longer have productive values, no longer think of what they give to humanity—they think of the pleasure, the entertainment they get, *to get them through the next terrible errors, of unreality*. We are a pleasure society! Look at us! Entertainment! Look at us! We are a nation of gamblers, not producers. Everybody is looking for money, for nothing, by gambling.

What do people do in states? The state's got a problem: "Bring in the gamblers." The states have a problem: "Legalize dope."

We are an entertainment society, an entertainment culture, in the same way, that Rome, with its Colosseum, its Circus Maximus, with the slaughter of Romans by Romans, under Emperors like Claudius, Nero, and so forth: *We have become that kind of sick culture. We have become a culture, in that generation, which has lost the moral fitness to survive.* They would rather die, than change their way of life. They would rather die, than give up their entertainment.

They will say, as I've written on a number of occasions: "I stole this stateroom, fair and square! And I'm not giving it up, even if this whole ship sinks!"

That is the idea: "I want my pleasure! I want my way of life! Don't try to make me rational! Don't ask me to behave rationally. *I need my entertainment! I've got to get through tonight!* And otherwise, if I have to face reality, I know I'm a piece of dung. And therefore, the only that keeps me from considering myself a piece of dung, is my pleasure! My entertainment, my diversion!"

You see these crazy models: If you take a dirty garment, you rip it to pieces, you put it on a naked, skinny girl, it's a high-fashion garment! This is the society we've become!

This is our problem.

EIRNS/Stuart Lewis

"Jesu, meine Freude": the challenging and beautiful eight-part motet by J.S. Bach which LaRouche has made an international anthem of his youth movement. A Youth Movement chorus performed in a "workshop" on the piece, while leaders including Megan Beets (at microphone) uncovered some of the secrets of its counterpoint. LaRouche's movement sings "Jesu" everywhere in its campaign organizing.

Qualities of Leadership

This is the same problem I addressed in Talladega, in pointing to the significance of Martin Luther King. Martin Luther King had a sense of immortality, which the people around him, including Jesse Jackson, didn't have. So, when Martin was killed (by courtesy of J. Edgar Hoover, or the wish of J. Edgar Hoover), what happened? The Civil Rights movement was fragmented. Why? Because leaders did not have the values that Martin had. Martin, as I said, had a sense of immortality: that life is a passage, from birth to death. There's nothing in it, that you can hold onto, except what you contribute by living. And therefore, it is what you are, immortally, which is what you are in life.

Now, every great leader in society, in a time of crisis, has been a leader precisely because they faced that reality. Not only because they had the talent to lead, but because they had the moral commitment, to say that "I can not be bought. You can not buy me, with my fear of death. But, I will lead."

The problem is, the pleasure society is the worst extreme of people, who *do not believe* in their children's future. The Baby-Boomers *do not believe in their children's future!* And that's what the children of the Baby-Boomers are saying! In their sense of hostility toward the Baby-Boomer generation: *"You have given us deliberately, a society which has no future!* You're asking us to live in a cage, where the animals aren't fed. And we don't like it. *We want you to change.*" They don't say, "We want to kill you." They haven't gotten to that point yet. That may come later. They say, *"We want you to change."* And, that's the conflict.

Learn the Lessons of History

If we can not change, if we select our choice of President, if we select our policies, now, in these weeks and months, the way things are going now, in general, *this nation will not long survive.* And *either way*, this system, that was consolidated, first in 1763, at the Treaty of Paris, proclaiming the victory, and establishment in fact, of a worldwide British Empire—intentionally modelled upon that of ancient Rome, an empire of a financier power, not legions—that empire has now come to its end. It will not survive. Either we will put it to a merciful conclusion, by a revival of the world economy, and bringing together a confederation of perfectly sovereign nation-states on this planet, around principles and issues of construction of the planet, and on promotion of development of the individual, within their national cultures, or we shall not survive.

We must do that.

We must not talk about the precedents of former history, as if they were legal precedents we must follow. We must talk about the *lessons* of former history, as I've indicated some of the lessons here, today, in brief. We must make a choice: We must say, the time for the way we have put humanity through brutal experiences in the past, must now finally come to an end."

We have, in our aspirations, and the founding of our republic, we've established the principle of the sovereign nation-state, as the most suitable form of government for a people. We have also understood, that all people have an interest, whether they recognize it yet, or not, in having such a form of state for themselves. We should understand, by now, that the principles of that sovereign state, are so common to us all, that despite the fact that we are separate and sovereign, we have a common interest, in a system of relations among sovereign states, which recognizes that principle reflected in our Declaration of Independence and Preamble of our Federal Constitution.

The time has come, when we need to have a new vision of leadership of this planet. A sense, we must now, for the sake of humanity, we must now create a global alliance, of respectively sovereign nation-states, committed to recovery, and committed to the principle of the immortality of the human individual. That the meaning of the individual lies, not merely in what happens between birth and death—which is a very short period of time on which to base a policy—but morality is based on a sense of what we, with our lives, with our talent, give to future generations; and to realizing the intentions of the generations before us: the kind of intention which enables us, if lived, to die with a smile on our face, that we have performed our mission, and it is good. And we are pleased.

Why do you think someone like Jeanne d'Arc would, knowing that she was going to be burned alive, if she did not compromise, would stick to her mission? If she had not continued her mission, the first modern nation-state, France, would not have come into existence. The Papacy would not have been restored, as it was. Modern society would not have come into existence, the modern nation-state. We'd be still living in some kind of feudal hell-hole.

She had a sense of *mission*, as all other great leaders of mankind have. And their sense of their interest in their *mission*, overrode the fears of mortality.

We need to select, and encourage, leadership of that kind. *With that kind of leadership*, and with insight which should be given to us by studying of the history of mankind from the past, we should understand the time has come for a change in the planet: the change to a system of sovereign nation-states, united by certain common ecumenical principles. We do not need to look forward to war. We will still need to maintain strategic defense. But, the transition to strategic defense, will be to a world in which war, as we've known it in the past, is no longer a necessary condition of mankind.

If we can do that, we shall survive. If we can not do that, we shall not survive. And if we can not do that, then we look forward in the early period, to a rate of mass death on this planet, from forces already set into motion, where the numbers of over 6 billion persons reported living today, will be reduced, fairly rapidly, to something significantly less than 1 billion.

We are looking at the brink of a precipitation into a New Dark Age, beyond anything that recorded history has given us before.

We have the option, the alternative, of moving upward again. And learning this lesson of the mistakes we've made, by taking steps to ensure these mistakes are not made again, then we can recover from the present situation.

That's the message of today. *And we have to make the choice, in the immediate days and weeks ahead. If we don't change, we are finished. We better start changing, now.*

Three Presidents

At the recently concluded Helsinki summit, President Trump stated:

> We (the United States and Russia) will have discussions on everything from trade to military to missiles to nuclear to China; we'll be talking a little bit about China (and) our mutual friend President Xi Jinping.

Consider where we are, where human history stands, at this moment. The Presidents—not Prime Ministers, but Presidents of sovereign republics—of the three most powerful nations on Earth are now, all three, working together. They have initiated a strategic engagement, a discussion among their three respective nations concerning the most vital issues facing humanity today. What we have witnessed so far is only the beginning of this dialogue, and if it continues and deepens, profound changes in the nature of human affairs are to be expected.

Consider what has been reported thus far regarding the personal rapport which Donald Trump has established with both Vladimir Putin and Xi Jinping, as well as the tangible steps which have been taken. There is one overriding characteristic to all of the initiatives we have seen during the 18 months that Donald Trump has been in office: a commitment to bring about a durable peace among the superpowers. This premier dedication is undeniable. Compare this to the directionality of world events during the preceding 16 years of the Bush and Obama presidencies—years of wars, regime change, NATO expansion, and other geopolitical atrocities.

In 1967, the great Pope Paul VI coined the phrase, "Development is the New Name for Peace." Truthful in its intention, the reverse is also true. Economic development which will serve the interests of mankind is only possible under conditions of peace and coopera-

tion. Despite the massive attacks on Donald Trump and the demonization of Vladimir Putin in the trans-Atlantic news media, this is now being achieved.

Ask yourself: Has anything like this ever before occurred in human history? Is it not completely unprecedented? Yes, there are earlier precedents, both those which were immediately successful in establishing a just peace, such as the Treaty of Westphalia, and intentions, such as John Quincy Adams' "Community of Principle Among Nations," but what we are witnessing today is of an entirely different character. What is very clear, from what has been said and done thus far, is that the three leaders are absolutely determined to end the era of British geopolitics—to place the relationships among nations on a completely different footing. This is exactly what Donald Trump said he was going to do during his campaign, and he is doing it.

Make no mistake. This is the greatest threat to the hegemony of the British financial empire in the entirety of its existence. What makes this fight winnable, is that in the combination of Russia, China and the United States we see a totality of power which has the means to see this reorientation of world affairs through. Alexander Hamilton and George Washington did not possess the power to dismantle the British Empire. Neither did Abraham Lincoln. FDR might have accomplished it, if he had lived, but even FDR lacked the strategic partners so crucial to such an undertaking. In the combination of Trump's America, Putin's Russia and Xi's China, a power exists to remake the world.

Do the British possess the means to defeat this? No, if the people of the United States enter the battle in increasing numbers to defend the Trump Presidency and push this process forward. It is true that the British possess dangerous weapons. They control the major news media; they currently have hegemony within the intelligence community; and they can deploy the financial power of the City of London and Wall Street. But they are up against the Presidents of the three most powerful nations on the planet. They are losing, and they are becoming more desperate.

Ending the Empire

Within this global battle, those individuals associated with Lyndon LaRouche have a specialized role—a decisive role—to play. We must not allow ourselves to be spectators.

Many people point to the events of 9/11, and the ensuing Afghanistan and Iraq wars, as the moment when the United States and Britain embarked on a global drive to isolate and destroy Russia, threaten and intimidate China, and cow the rest of the world into submission. But if we are to succeed in the current battle, it is necessary to extend our vision and to go back further—to understand and correct grievous errors made during an earlier period.

In 1971 Lyndon LaRouche was practically alone in his economic forecasts, in identifying the disastrous global consequences of the decision by Richard Nixon in terminating the Bretton Woods monetary agreements and ending the system of "fixed exchange rates." In 1975, LaRouche proposed his remedy to the colossal error of the Nixon presidency—the International Development Bank. Everything we have witnessed during the last four and one-half decades in terms of economic crisis, mass poverty and warfare has resulted from the failure on the part of government leaders to act on LaRouche's warnings and proposals.

Donald Trump, Vladimir Putin and Xi Jinping all desire world peace. They all want economic development which will benefit the people of their own and other nations. The only way to secure this—to ensure this—is to follow "the wise words of Lyndon LaRouche" in the weeks and months ahead. Specifically, governments must reexamine LaRouche's proposal for a New Bretton Woods agreement, one which will end—for good—the era of financial speculation, one which will shatter the power of the offshore banks, vulture funds and other financial parasites, and one which will put the economic and monetary relations among nations on a secure footing, such that stable long-term investment in physical economic projects becomes the norm.

It is time to end the era of usury and predatory financial speculation. The nations of China, Russia and the United States have the combined power to accomplish this. That is why the British are howling.

Has an opportunity like this ever come before in human history? Shall this opportunity be fulfilled? The answer—the realization of this potential—lies with us. Our clarity of intent and determined intervention will make the difference.